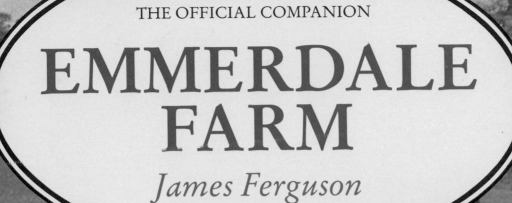

THE OFFICIAL COMPANION

EMMERDALE FARM

James Ferguson

WEIDENFELD AND NICOLSON · LONDON

BY ARRANGEMENT WITH YORKSHIRE TELEVISION LIMITED

Series created by Kevin Laffan.

Executive Producer   Keith Richardson
Producer   Stuart Doughty
Story Editor   Andrew Holden
Script Editor   David Lane

Published in Great Britain by
George Weidenfeld & Nicolson Limited
91 Clapham High Street
London SW4 7TA

Printed in Great Britain by
Butler & Tanner Ltd, Frome and London

Contents

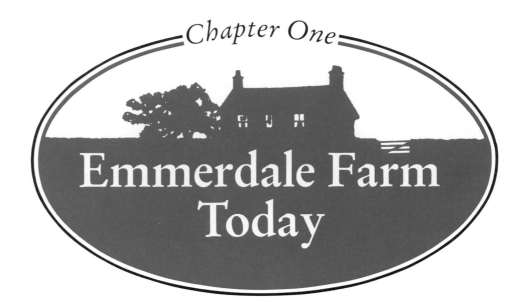

Chapter One

Emmerdale Farm Today

When Stuart Doughty was appointed Producer of 'Emmerdale Farm' in January 1988, after producing Channel 4's 'Brookside', he inherited a basic set of characters and a story setting which had been created more than fifteen years earlier. In that time, 'Emmerdale Farm' had progressed from a programme which was shown only in the Yorkshire TV and Tyne-Tees TV regions, to a highly popular serial which is now screened simultaneously twice weekly throughout the ITV network, as well as being shown in many countries in Europe and elsewhere overseas.

'Emmerdale Farm' was not devised as a 'soap' opera, however. When it first appeared, it was to be a drama series which was shown for a limited period each year with a long break in the summer and a two-week break at Christmas. It was not originally planned to continue for more than twenty-six weeks, but its popularity did result in several series, each beginning after the summer break and ending the following spring, albeit with a Christmas break.

In comparison with other programmes of this type, 'Emmerdale Farm' has been slow to develop. Instead of being designed as a bi-weekly programme aimed immediately at a mass audience and then thrust into prominence at peak viewing times, it started slowly as a regional drama series with a very localised viewing public.

It took several years for it to develop into what might be termed a soap opera but even that name is not strictly accurate. However, it does loosely fit into that category because it features a drama with a recognisable set of characters in a continuing setting of a farm and a village; there is a family unit surrounded by other characters who represent varying aspects of our society and who experience the problems of living within a modern Britain, albeit in a strikingly beautiful countryside setting.

This gradual development is reflected in the remarkably low turn-over of the 'Emmerdale' cast. Five of the original members are still with the serial and are playing characters who were established in the very first episode; a sixth (Toke Townley), died in 1984 while continuing his role of Grandad Pearson, and one of the original characters (Jack Sugden) remained in the series until 1988, although he was played by a second actor. Clive Hornby took over as Jack from Andrew Burt.

8

This long-term retention of characters is unusual for any soap opera and it reflects the durability of the serial combined with the friendliness that is generated both on screen and off. All members of the cast are friends with one another and with the production team, and this is one of the remarkable qualities of the programme.

But even a serial as well established as 'Emmerdale Farm' must not be allowed to stagnate. It must keep pace with life in the latter years of the twentieth century and it must cater for a changing audience.

As Stuart Doughty said, 'We need evolution, not revolution. My job is not to change "Emmerdale Farm" so that it resembles something like "EastEnders" or "Brookside" but to make sure that the characters and the story develop in keeping with the times in which we live while remaining faithful to the Yorkshire rural background. We've got to be up-to-date with farming procedures too, and able to portray the effects of matters like the EEC rulings, the difficulties of coping with milk quotas and the growing need for farmers to diversify.

'At the same time, we can't ignore the other soaps; we have to be competitive even though each soap has a different appeal and attracts different viewers.'

Stuart knows that most members of the 'Emmerdale Farm' audience are over thirty-five years old, with many being over fifty-five years of age.

But younger viewers – the audience of the future – are also discovering the delights of 'Emmerdale Farm' and in order to attract them, more younger characters have been introduced over the last few years.

Emmerdale Farm is set in rich pastures on the slopes of a Yorkshire Dale.

9

This famous and familiar view of the sun setting over Emmerdale Farm is featured on the opening titles sequence.

To keep that new audience, the story must keep up-to-date, it must generate interest and it must introduce new characters. When Anne Gibbons was producer (1979–83) she introduced a whole range of new and permanent characters including the Merricks and Alan Turner. She realised that, in order to develop, 'Emmerdale Farm' needed more of the serial element. It should not depend on shorter storylines involving characters who appeared in some six episodes and then disappeared from the story, but it needed stronger, more permanent characters about whom a powerful and continuing drama could be written.

Young actors and actresses are introduced so that the audience can follow the characters through to maturity, and this benefits the acting profession too, by giving young artistes a wonderful opportunity to learn their craft and to mature with the guidance and friendship of some very experienced and capable members of the 'Emmerdale Farm' cast.

However, some of the cast acknowledge that security of the kind created by a long-running drama serial can be strange for anyone in the acting profession; many work spasmodically and find the long-term peace of mind somewhat unsettling!

But successive producers of 'Emmerdale Farm' have accepted that artistes wish to move ahead in their careers and so the producers have always been willing to accommodate these needs by writing characters out of the serial – and even writing them back in if necessary!

Stuart Doughty stressed the point that although 'Emmerdale Farm' is unique among British soaps for its wealth of outdoor locations, it is not a travelogue about the Yorkshire Dales, nor is it a programme about farming. It is a drama serial about people living in Britain at the present time, and the continuing story must revolve around the central characters, a view echoed by successive producers. Furthermore, the viewers must feel they know the characters, and those characters must be of continuing interest in the way they cope with life. In the case of 'Emmerdale Farm', they happen to live in Yorkshire.

Even so, the programme is not about the location in which 'Emmerdale Farm' is set, but about the people who live and work in and around Beckindale. This view is reinforced by Richard Handford who was the producer from July 1983 until the end of June 1986. At that time he accelerated the pace of 'Emmerdale Farm' by including more scenes within each half-hour episode and by strengthening the central characters. One incident which caused the viewing figures to rise, and the letters of complaint to flow, was Jack Sugden's first extra-marital affair.

While married to Pat, Jack had an affair with Karen Moore, a romance which brought a mixed bag of accusations and compliments. The accusations suggested that Jack would never do such a thing and that this was not a suitable story for 'Emmerdale Farm', while others felt it gave the serial a much-needed boost.

In fact, around this time, the viewing figures for 'Emmerdale Farm' reached No. 3 out of the nation's top twenty programmes from both the BBC and ITV.

Stuart Doughty is aware of criticism that 'Emmerdale Farm' is rather slow moving and that nothing much happens; he regards this as unfair because a lot does happen. As he points out, 'No good drama is slow and sleepy; and "Emmerdale Farm" is a good drama serial, as its record proves. But the pace of events in Beckindale will never be as rapid as in "EastEnders" – this is a different world and the events must therefore reflect the true life of the region.'

He went on, 'In "Emmerdale Farm", we will not include social issues for their own sake, nor will we seek to preach to our viewers, but we will include any subject which is relevant to "Emmerdale Farm". In recent months, we have included addiction to pain killers, unemployment, economical changes to the land, ecology, the dumping of nuclear waste, feminism and the problems of village communities coming to terms with the changes that result from increasing leisure time and tourism, such as caravan sites and the problems of conservation.'

He added that there is no subject which cannot be covered in 'Emmerdale

The stars of 'Emmerdale Farm' during their 1988 publicity campaign in London. Left to right: *Frazer Hines (Joe), Hugh Manning (the Rev. Donald Hinton), Sheila Mercier (Annie Sugden), Ronald Magill (Amos Brearly), Stan Richards (Seth Armstrong).*

Farm', although it must be borne in mind that the audience views the programme at 6.30pm. 'Emmerdale Farm' will never impose its views on controversial matters, although highly topical themes will be presented in the form of drama so that the viewers can make their own judgements.

Recent examples include the morality of investing in trees for tax avoidance reasons or the problems of young people seeking employment as experienced through the characters of Nick Bates and Archie Brooks. Aspects of conservation are shown sympathetically through the eyes of Henry Wilks while the efforts of Dolly and Kathy to establish their own farm shop owe something to the feminist movement; the plight of agricultural workers is shown through the eyes of Jock MacDonald and Seth Armstrong. One of Jackie Merrick's romances was with an Asian girl, but that caused resentment from her father, not on the grounds of colour but because of the social class of Jackie's family.

It must always be remembered that the characters in 'Emmerdale Farm' are gentler than those in 'EastEnders' and would not often get involved in problems associated with city life, but their problems are just as real and just as important.

Within the future it could be expected that the fictitious Beckindale may experience an influx of commuters from the cities, even as far away as London.

With electrification of the main-line rail routes between Yorkshire and the south, there will be more incomers – this will result in more country cottages being purchased with a correspondingly high increase in their prices to the detriment of young Dales people who will be unable to afford them. And it

Henry Wilks (Arthur Pentelow) and Amos Brearly behind the bar of the Woolpack Inn, Beckindale, doing what they do best!

During the celebrations for the 1000th episode, Eamonn Andrews sprung a 'This is Your Life' surprise on Sheila Mercier.

can be assured that any new characters will generate more drama, romance and interest.

There might be the question of exploitation of the Dales because southern business people are showing an interest in Yorkshire as an area rich in quarrying potential, especially for limestone, or as an area of afforestation or mass tourism. The Dales could become a playground for the wealthy, or they could become a dormitory area for those seeking refuge from the cities. The effect upon the residents would be momentous.

Keith Richardson joined 'Emmerdale Farm' as Executive Producer in 1986 although he had been Unit Manager for the very first episode in 1972. His role is to act as overseer for the entire production and he is not involved in the day-to-day running of the serial; that is the producer's job. However, Mr Richardson does help to overcome any production problems that might arise, and he attends meetings when the policy and long-term storyline are discussed. The storyline is often determined as much as a year in advance. He and the producer establish the general direction of the story and the continuing role of the characters.

He is aware of the criticism which suggests that 'Emmerdale Farm' is slightly old-fashioned but much of this is due to the inheritance of the three main locations which have been focal points of the story since the first episode – the farm, the village and the studio. During the coming years he intends to make more use of lightweight cameras and modern outside broadcast equipment with the aim of recording more scenes on location. It is widely recognised that the superb scenery in which the Beckindale stories are recorded is a bonus which none of the other competing dramas can boast. Mr Richardson believes this should be used to its greatest advantage. Michael Russell said that the scenery distinguishes 'Emmerdale Farm' from other serials, while Anne Gibbons said that it marked a huge 'plus' for the programme. Michael Glynn, producer from 1976 to 1979, believes the countryside helps to reflect the manner in which the characters live and work, and Richard Handford confirmed that when the programmes reduced their outside broadcast sequences, the audiences began to dwindle.

Today's lighter and more manœuvrable cameras and sound equipment

13

ensure that more use of the Yorkshire countryside is a distinct possibility and Keith Richardson hopes this will generate a more spontaneous atmosphere in the recorded scenes. He is aware, however, that 'Emmerdale Farm' does have a loyal and faithful following, a dedicated cast and highly professional production crew. Any major changes will have to be introduced gradually and with sympathy and care.

The advance of time and technology means that these changes will come but they will be gentle – in keeping with the pace of the programme.

'One of the things that pleases me greatly,' said Keith Richardson, 'is that when "Emmerdale Farm" was shown at the same time as the BBC's "EastEnders", "Emmerdale" won the higher ratings. "Emmerdale Farm" is now shown at 6.30pm on all ITV regions, and features in the top ten ITV ratings. It is being shown to a London audience at this time, having moved from 5.15pm, and so we are winning a whole new city audience.'

To attract more viewers from London and the south, a highly successful poster campaign was launched on London's Underground network in May 1988, when the joy of visiting 'Emmerdale Farm' and the Beckindale countryside through the medium of television was hailed as 'Fresh Air on the Tube' or 'Country Breaks. Every week.'

The increasing interest in the countryside in general and the Yorkshire Dales in particular means that the family of 'Emmerdale Farm' and the people of Beckindale represent thousands who live and work in this fascinating region. Through the programme, the values, traditions, character and sheer beauty of the Yorkshire Dales are freely shared with millions.

In whatever way the future affects the Yorkshire Dales or the British countryside and its people, it will continue to be reflected in the continuing story of the characters of 'Emmerdale Farm'.

Realism in 'Emmerdale Farm'

The strength of 'Emmerdale Farm' lies in its gritty realism which comes from the use of genuine Yorkshire Dales backgrounds such as the farm, which becomes Emmerdale Farm, and the village, which becomes Beckindale. Half of the programme is recorded in the studios and half is recorded out of doors; no other British soap opera makes such extensive use of the countryside and every-day locations. The farm and the village are utilised throughout the serial but the regular use of additional outdoor locations serves to maintain the sense of reality. These have included scenes at York and Wetherby Races, the limestone caves of the Dales, a local trout farm, the beautiful house used as Home Farm, Forestry Commission land, the Great Yorkshire Show, Kilnsey Show, Otley Market and many other rural locations, as well as towns like Harrogate, York and Wetherby, and the beach at Bridlington. On one occasion, Fred Trueman, the noted England cricketer and fast bowler, appeared as himself in a scene.

Another well-known face was actor and comedian Max Wall. He was brought in to play an old friend of Grandad Pearson's, a First World War

Joe competing in the fell race at Kilnsey.

Left: *Fred Trueman, the England and Yorkshire fast bowler and all-round cricketer, played himself in an episode of 'Emmerdale Farm'.*

Above: *One of the famous faces to appear in 'Emmerdale Farm' was comedian Max Wall. He played an old wartime comrade of Sam Pearson's who had returned for an emotional reunion.*

comrade, and the two old men enjoyed a reunion. In real life Toke Townley, who played Sam Pearson, had always admired the work of Max Wall and for him any scene he played with Max would be cherished. When the time came to record the sequences, the countryside was covered in thick snow and this worried the producer, Michael Glynn.

He was concerned about the health and welfare of the two old men, for they had to climb a hillside in thick snow. But, clad in dry, warm clothes and Wellington boots, they set off in their role as two old comrades, Toke thoroughly enjoying his moments with Max Wall. And they disappeared over the hill in the snow, friends now and two very happy old characters.

But it is the farm we know as Emmerdale Farm, the village we know as Beckindale, the inn we know as the Woolpack and the beautiful countryside in which they are situated, which are the true stars. Selection of the farm was the task of the first director of the series, Gordon Fleming. He had to find a suitable village to represent Beckindale, and a genuine farm which would fulfil the role of the fictitious Emmerdale. He chose Arncliffe as the village, now relinquished in favour of another setting, but the farm he selected at the beginning, in 1972, continues in its role. It is a real working farm; the cows, sheep, equipment, house, buildings and fields all belong to the resident farmer and his family, only becoming the Sugdens' farm when 'borrowed' for the purpose. The realistic atmosphere which emerges in the way the characters dress, talk, live and work is due to Gordon's own experience, even down to the furnishings of Annie's kitchen. Evacuated to the Highlands of Scotland from Glasgow during the war, Gordon lived on a farm and those childhood memories have been faithfully captured in Emmerdale's authentic background. The trappings of a middle-class life style would never appear on a Dales farm.

The real farm is a typical Dales mixed holding of around 200 acres where Farmer Bell grows hay, silage and 30 acres of barley. The entire holding is worked by Arthur Bell and his son Trevor, and they also breed prize-winning Masham sheep and fat lambs while maintaining a herd of superb Friesian dairy cows. These are the animals which are seen on our screens along with the hens, ducks, geese and a Border collie sheepdog called Dyne which occasionally sneaks into the picture. This is *not* Matt's sheepdog, Nell, who is hired for the purpose.

But if Jack Sugden is seen milking a cow, he is genuinely doing so, just as Matt will help a ewe to give birth to her lamb and Jackie will tend a new-born calf. Farmer Bell has taught the actors those essential skills and it is true-to-life moments like these which blend so well with the fictitious story of Emmerdale Farm. This does not happen every day; it happens only when required by Yorkshire Television and when this location is needed for forthcoming instalments of the story.

Right from the start of the 'Emmerdale Farm' programmes, Yorkshire TV assured the owner that the real name and location of the farm, and the name of its occupants, would never be revealed by them. That pledge has been strictly honoured, even down to referring to the farmer and his wife as Farmer Arthur Bell and Mrs Bell, which is not their real name.

But in spite of Yorkshire Television's promise, the secret has been discovered by ardent viewers who have shown a remarkable capacity for detecting this

A firm friendship has grown between the real farmer and his wife, and the cast of 'Emmerdale Farm'. Here Mr and Mrs Arthur Bell examine some sheep with Annie Sugden and Matt Skilbeck (Fred Pyne).

quiet location. As a result, coach tours and motorists now drive to the vicinity of the farm so that passengers can peer over the hedges from a distance in the hope of seeing the Sugdens, the Skilbecks and the other characters. They are often disappointed, for these well-known characters are on the farm only when recording is taking place – and even when recording is taking place, they are usually lost among the crowd which forms the production team.

Any visitors who are tempted to call at the farm should remember that this is private property; the farmer and his family do not form any part of the programme. If mention of this seems superfluous, it is a sad fact that some viewers do call without invitation – one day, 150 people arrived in Arthur's farm yard expecting to see the Sugdens. Happily, Arthur is a model of patience even though some tourists have been thoughtless enough to call at all hours, knocking on the door or even entering the private kitchen without invitation, expecting to see Annie and members of her family.

As Arthur said, 'We get on very well with the television crew and the cast, but some tourists can be a nuisance. They forget this is a working farm, and that it's our private house. Some even spy on us with binoculars! It's only a few, but they can spoil things for the others.'

One fact that puzzles most sightseers is that this farm is about seven miles from the village which features as Beckindale. The illusion of the farm being in Beckindale is achieved through careful camera work and skilful editing of the tapes. In this way, the marvellous marriage of fact and fiction continues into the village of Beckindale.

On the edge of that village, however, there is another farm which is sometimes thought to be Emmerdale; it is situated near the end of the street which contains the inn used as the Woolpack but this is *not* the one which features as Emmerdale.

Just as a real farm is used as Emmerdale, so a real Yorkshire Dales village is used as Beckindale; this tiny community has a real inn, a real church, real village hall, real vicar, real post-office-cum-shop and above all, real people who go about their daily lives.

Once every month or so, their peaceful way of life is interrupted by a fleet of Yorkshire TV Outside Broadcast vehicles. They arrive with lots of private cars, a canteen vehicle and seemingly endless miles of cables with dozens of people at the end of them. For most of that particular day and the four or five that follow, this village is transformed into Beckindale. And in addition to the production team, there will be the familiar faces of the cast whose presence is so well known on screen. Another factor, which is due entirely to the success of the serial, is the volume of tourists and sightseers.

Each year, tens of thousands of them arrive by coach and car to watch the

The Woolpack Inn, Beckindale, so typical of a Yorkshire Dales inn. There is always a friendly welcome here.

recording and (hopefully) to meet their screen favourites. Even though the village is now a prime target for tourists, it remains delightfully unspoilt.

This is not the first 'Beckindale', however. When the 'Emmerdale Farm' series first appeared, another Yorkshire Dales village was selected and used for about five years. That was Arncliffe which is in Littondale, an off-shoot of Upper Wharfedale in the North Yorkshire Dales. Gordon Fleming, as director of the first seven episodes, wanted to give the feeling of open space and a true Dales atmosphere; as he had a limited time to record each outside broadcast, the correct village setting was so important. The limited time scale and the beautiful scenery of Arncliffe provided a freshness that has never been lost. Arthur Mee described Arncliffe as 'deep set like a jewel between the wooded slopes of the moors and fells'. It rests in a beautiful setting, but it soon became evident that Arncliffe was too far from the studios in Leeds. This increased the time involved in shooting the external scenes, a lot of the time being taken up with travelling from the studios. Indeed, in those early days, the cast and crew often stayed overnight in local hotels. And so in 1976 Yorkshire TV discovered another delightful village, another jewel among trees in a hollow between two major cities with the rising fells not far away.

With a population of only 359, their chosen village was a mere seven miles from the studio and it had one pub, one church, one shop – and Europe's largest sewage treatment works. They are in the grounds of the former Stansfield Hall and Estate; the Hall was built in the eighteenth century by Sir Walter Calverley and it was he who constructed most of the tenants' cottages in the village.

The estate and its sewage treatment works are now administered by Yorkshire Water while most of the property in the village is owned by Bradford Metropolitan District Council. It was a poster issued by the Council in an attempt to attract tourists that revealed to the world the setting for Beckindale. But who would dare to describe the lovely setting for Beckindale as a council estate in one of West Yorkshire's major industrial cities?

When Yorkshire TV declared they would like to use this village, they called a meeting of the council and all the residents to seek their views. Having explained their purpose and the problems that would follow, Yorkshire TV were delighted to find 100% agreement to their proposal – and so this tiny village became the fictional Beckindale. Inevitably, there are occasional minor grumbles from the residents – such as when they cannot drive down the street because of the tumble of cables, or walk to the post office without pushing through the mass of people that form the production crew. But these are all good-natured mutterings.

But as Arthur Pickles, caretaker of the village institute said, 'You should never buy a house next to the sewage works and then complain about the smell!'

When cottages in this village become empty, the council sells them, so new people are moving in and not all of them appreciate the disruption that occurs when 'Emmerdale Farm' is being recorded.

But Marion Smith, a verger at the tiny parish church, has lived in the village for over fifty years and says, 'We're all on first-name terms with the actors and television people – they're no trouble. It's the tourists who cause problems –

Marion Smith is the verger for the church and has lived in the village for more than 50 years. She welcomes the presence of the recording team when 'Emmerdale Farm' turns her village into Beckindale.

picking flowers from our gardens or peering through our windows. They forget this is a real village with real people.'

Sam and Jennifer Thrippleton have a delightful tea-room and photo gallery at the Old Hall from where they sell official 'Emmerdale Farm' souvenirs while offering refreshments. Sam says that 'Emmerdale Farm' has given new life and prosperity to the village and this is something about which none of the original villagers complains. Sam and Jennifer are steeped in the history of 'Emmerdale', and in the grounds of the Old Hall are the remains of a sixteenth-century moat, complete with water; it was into this that a bull once chased Amos! Their home was the fictional home of Harry Mowlem, Emmerdale's first murder victim, and one of the walls in a barn is whitewashed, a relic of an early recording session in this village when the whiteness was needed to increase the light in the dark barn.

The walls of the tea-room are rich with photographs of the stars and the locations, with life-size photographs of some of the characters and a whole range of souvenirs of 'Emmerdale Farm'.

For anyone entering the village, there is little on the streets to indicate that this is the setting for Beckindale, other than a familiar view along the main street with its post office and local inn. The inn is called the Commercial and the buses have destination boards for places like Bradford, Shipley and Guiseley. But on the days when recording takes place, there is a vital transformation. Yorkshire TV's carpenters and scenery experts arrive before recording commences and transform the Commercial Inn into the Woolpack.

The name of the Commercial Inn is covered by a sign saying 'The Woolpack Inn', and there is added a nicely painted inn sign depicting sheep and packs of their fleeces, with a further one hailing 'Ephraims Skipdale Ales, established 1778'. A notice above the front door proclaims 'Amos Brearly – Licensed to sell by retail, tobacco and intoxicating liquors to be consumed on or off the premises'. This illusion is completed by the appearance of 'Emmerdale Farm' vehicles in the car park outside, such as Matt and Dolly's new vehicle, Phil Pearce's battered old van or the Home Farm Estate Range Rover.

But inside, the inn is not like the Woolpack. Landlord Bryan Hirst says that this is the Commercial Inn, not the Woolpack, and it is his livelihood, not Henry's and Amos's.

He does agree, however, that many fans who enter the Commercial Inn do so in the hope of finding Amos and Henry behind the bar and he cheerfully admits that this is good for his own sales of beer. It is not unusual for several coach loads of people to be queueing at the bar and for the queue to stretch into the street.

When visitors persist in asking for Amos or Henry, Bryan says they've had a busy day and they're upstairs resting. This happens a lot during recording sessions which take place just outside, when the exterior becomes that of the Woolpack Inn and the street is peopled by the characters of 'Emmerdale Farm' and Beckindale.

Another surprise for callers is that the inside of the inn is not at all like the interior of the Woolpack; the Woolpack's bar is to be found only in the studio at Leeds. Opposite the pub is the village post-office-cum-shop, surely the tiniest of business premises. It sells everything from stamps to soft drinks, and

the proprietor Ian French said that sometimes the interior of his shop is used in the programme, although the exterior with its village telephone kiosk and Victorian post box, is much more familiar.

The church is another building which features on our screens. Now served from a neighbouring parish, it provides an atmospheric setting for baptisms and funerals, as well as the annual Christmas carol service – and who can forget the emotion and joy of Kathy and Jackie Merrick's wedding?

When not featuring in recordings, there may be a life-size cardboard cut-out of the Beckindale vicar, Rev. Donald Hinton, outside the church door. Tourists can take a photograph of their friends at his side – and in return are asked to make a small donation for the upkeep of the church or for some other charity. In this way, the church benefits from 'Emmerdale Farm'.

The village hall is often used, for its clean interior provides the facilities for all kinds of indoor settings; when not featuring in the programme, it serves as a place of refreshment for the cast and production crew, and also offers a make-up salon and dressing rooms. As a location for the programme, it is well known as the venue of Beckindale's annual Christmas pantomime and as a setting for meetings of various sorts. One example occurred when Alan Turner

The Rev. Arthur Wilson used to live in the village which features as Beckindale. Here he is with a life-like figure of the Rev. Donald Hinton, Vicar of Beckindale.

21

A photograph from the Sugden family album. It shows the christening of Matt and Peggy's twins, Samuel and Sarah (Sam and Sally) in Beckindale Parish Church. In the picture from left to right are Grandad Sam Pearson (Toke Townley), Sally, Annie Sugden, the vicar of Beckindale, the Reverend Edward Ruskin (George Little), Sam, Joe Sugden, Matt Skilbeck and Peggy Skilbeck. Peggy died soon after their birth and the twins were later killed in a road accident.

attempted to lecture to the Skipdale Chamber of Commerce, but was defeated by a sore throat; those light-hearted sequences were shot in this village hall.

To add to the illusion of reality, more village buildings are used in the series and they include the exterior of some cottages, in particular, those ostensibly occupied by Mrs Bates, Joe Sugden and Seth Armstrong, that of Mrs Bates being opposite the pub while the latter two live in Demdyke Row. Of course, there is no Demdyke Row although a remarkably similar row of cottages does exist in the real village. The interiors of these pretty cottages are created in the studio. Even so, some visitors do believe they are occupied by Beckindale folk.

To complete the metamorphosis from true Dales village to Beckindale, when the local bus comes along, its destination board will show either Beckindale or Hotten. This bus is hired from the West Yorkshire Car Company's Depot in Harrogate and attracts curious glances as it motors to the location with 'Beckindale' on its destination board.

The most fascinating aspect of this merging of fact and fiction is the manner in which the life of this village goes on around the cameras and dramas being enacted in its main street. Customers come to the pub for a meal and a drink, even if it has the Woolpack Inn's name on the outside. Inside, it is the Commercial Inn and business must go on.

The travelling library halts awhile and so does the real service bus; villagers pop into the shop or post their letters and the near-by farm goes about its daily routine. There might be some confusion to visitors on a Sunday afternoon each August because that is when the cast and production team of 'Emmerdale Farm' play a charity cricket match in the village. The 'Beckindale' team plays

against the local cricket club to raise money for charity but it is also an indication of the friendship and rapport that exists between the village and the production team.

Meanwhile, in the background to all these events, whether real or fictional, a cockerel crows and the sound is sometimes caught by the recording team – yet another touch of authenticity.

But this is not a cockerel from 'Emmerdale Farm' acting in a scene – it is a real one in a real farm yard in a real village which assumes a famous role for our pleasure.

When working on their allotments, there's always competition between Seth and Amos.

Chapter Two

From the Beginning

'Emmerdale Farm' was Britain's first-ever lunchtime TV drama serial, popularly called a soap opera. Today, the word 'soap' is used to describe this and other serials like 'Coronation Street', 'Dallas' or 'EastEnders', although in strict terms neither 'Emmerdale Farm' nor any of the other long-running British serials are soap operas. A genuine soap opera should be transmitted every day whereas 'Emmerdale Farm' is screened twice weekly.

The original soaps date to the 1930s when American manufacturers of soap and soap powders decided to sponsor radio serials to attract massive audiences of women. It was felt that the supporting advertisements would persuade the listeners to buy their products and that a huge audience would result in very profitable sales. These soap operas, as they became known, were an immediate success; they portrayed events and life-styles far removed from those who listened to the continuing stories. Their success generated a whole new field of popular entertainment which attracted a mass audience. In England, when the only radio network was the BBC (without advertisements), a long-running radio serial began on 5 January 1948 – it was called 'Mrs Dale's Diary', later known as 'The Dales', and this ended in 1969. Another popular radio serial was 'The Archers' which started on 1 January 1951 and is still running.

But it was not until the 1960s that British television realised the entertainment value of soap operas. None the less, the BBC had started one – 'The Groves' – as early as April 1954, and then on 9 December 1960 'Coronation Street' was first transmitted and it has now become Britain's longest-running TV serial. The BBC followed with 'Compact' in January 1962, which ran twice weekly until 1965 when the BBC introduced 'United' and then 'The Newcomers'. ATV followed with 'Emergency Ward 10' and another newcomer was a motel-based soap called 'Crossroads' which started in November 1964 and concluded in the spring of 1988.

The range of commercial TV companies which had been created after 1955 also realised the entertainment value and the commercial potential of the long-running drama serial. When the permitted hours of transmission were extended, an entirely new and very substantial day-time audience was created. Lunchtime television viewing had come to Britain.

Yorkshire Television now considered the transmission of a long-running

serial designed to attract lunchtime viewers. If it was to fit the format of the so-called soap operas, it would require very definite locations and interesting characters around whom continuing stories could be woven. The characters would have to represent a wide selection of people, including working class and professional class, and, above all, the proposed serial would have to have a strong sense of reality.

The lives it portrayed would also have to be very realistic. If it was to appear on the screens at lunchtime, it would require a strong dramatic content, albeit laced with social problems, domestic gossip, perhaps some informative sequences about a particular way of life but, most important of all, it would have to reflect the daily lives of either a community or a family. A strong feminine interest was necessary and the viewers would have to feel that they were actually sharing the lives of the characters, laughing with them, crying with them, sympathising with them, loving some and hating others, being privy to some of their secrets and observing their delicate personal relationships and their interaction with one another. The viewers would have to become involved, even to the extent of feeling they were 'friends' with some of the characters.

The task of creating the all-important foundations for the proposed new series fell upon the distinguished author and playwright, Kevin Laffan. With

Jack Sugden (Clive Hornby) harvesting at Emmerdale Farm.

25

Kevin Laffan

several West End stage successes to his credit, including *It's a Two Feet Six Inches Above the Ground World*, and an impressive list of TV plays to his name, he had had experience as an actor and as a Director of Production at the Everyman Theatre in Reading. With his valuable experience, Mr Laffan was asked to draft the first episodes and to establish the family of central characters and those who lives they affected.

At that stage it was anticipated that the new serial would run for only a short time, no more than twenty-six episodes and not longer than two years, but as Kevin Laffan worked on this basic idea, he realised that the impressive countryside of the Yorkshire Dales would provide a magnificent setting for the serial, and that the people who lived and worked there would provide a range of fascinating characters.

Gradually, the idea emerged. He decided on a farming background, not a gentleman's farm but a small Dales holding where life was tough and simple, and where a widow and her growing family had to cope without their recently dead father. But it was not as simple as that. The children of that family had to have strong personalities too; there had to be drama, tragedy and love in their lives. Other characters were required and so the farm had to be close to a village which provided the family's recreation and supplied basic essentials. People would live and work in that village, Dales people with their own problems and relationships with one another.

And as Kevin Laffan worked, the Sugden family was created. The new widow was Annie, alone after the death of her husband, Jacob. But Jacob had not been a good man for the farm – he had been work-shy and had drunk away most of its profits, so the farm was in a sorry state, badly maintained and run-down with a bleak future. It had been unpromising when he was alive but the prospects were dismal following Jacob's death.

Annie had two sons, Jack who was something of a rebel and a dreamer, a prodigal son in many ways, and Joe, the baby of the family who was named after his paternal grandfather. Joe felt there was more to a young man's life than working on a Dales farm. There was Peggy too, Annie and Jacob's daughter and a sensible sister for both Jack and Joe. She was married to the slow-thinking, slow-moving farm labourer who worked for the Sugdens. He was Matt Skilbeck, reliable and loyal to the Sugdens, a typical countryman in many ways.

The older generation was represented by Annie's father who lived with the family on the farm; he was Mr Sam Pearson, a widower, who was a God-fearing, church-going Dalesman of the kind found in former days and whose philosophy was based on the old country ways which were rich with the traditions and lore of farming and village life.

In the village, the centre of gossip and recreation was the pub and here Mr Laffan created a landlord by the name of Amos Brearly, originally intended to be a minor character in the series, while the professional classes were represented by Henry Wilks, a prematurely retired wool dyer from Bradford who, following the death of his wife, had come to live in a large house called Inglebrook on the outskirts of the village. To the unchanging folk of the dale, he appeared as something of an intruder for in real life commuters from the cities had then started to live in the Dales villages.

Andrew Burt was the first actor to play Jack Sugden.

A vicar was required for the church and there would be other essential village characters such as a shopkeeper, poacher and others who entered the story from time to time. Further characters could be introduced to the story when they were required. On the outskirts of the village was the Verney Estate, with Mr George Verney as squire. When he died, his nephew, Gerald (a London businessman), could not afford to keep the estate because of death duties, so it was sold to NY Estates.

Mr Laffan called his village Beckindale, a name which is so apt for the Yorkshire Dales, and he named the pub the Woolpack, a popular name in the region. Other venues include the near-by market town of Hotten, the village of Connelton and the Dales town of Skipdale, the district's commercial centre. This combination of a potentially powerful storyline, with the bonus of some magnificent countryside, had all the hallmarks of a successful serial, and the first episode, written by Kevin Laffan, produced by David Goddard and directed by Gordon Fleming, was transmitted by Yorkshire Television on Monday, 16 October 1972 with title music composed by Tony Hatch.

The opening episode contained the funeral of Jacob Sugden and the viewers saw his cortège winding through the lanes to Beckindale Parish Church, and some viewers will recall the characters who attended that funeral – Annie Sugden (Sheila Mercier) in the traditional black of a widow, her father Sam Pearson (Toke Townley) with his black coat and white scarf (the splash of white being a custom at some Yorkshire funerals).

A scene from the first episode of 'Emmerdale Farm'. Jacob Sugden has died and his family mourn after his funeral. In this historic picture are (from left to right) *Joe Sugden, Matt and Peggy Skilbeck, Jack Sugden, Annie Sugden and Sam Pearson.*

There was also the surly Jack (Andrew Burt). Unable or perhaps unwilling to get on with either his father or his younger brother, he had left home eight years earlier at the age of eighteen and had never been heard of since. And now, in this first episode, he had unexpectedly come home for the funeral of his father, but it was soon to be revealed that Jacob had left Emmerdale Farm to Jack. It had always been a Dales tradition that a farmer left his business to the eldest son. Jack was soon to experience the deep resentment felt by his brother Joe and his sister, Peggy. Both had worked hard to keep the farm going during Jack's absence and Jacob's mismanagement.

At first the family did not know of Jack's presence at the funeral, but afterwards he returned to Emmerdale Farm to join his mourning family and to make peace with his mother, his sister Peggy (Jo Kendall) and his young brother Joe (Frazer Hines). His reception was far from warm. Peggy was married to Matt Skilbeck (Freddie Pyne), who provided the calm reassurance they all needed at that moment. Incidentally, the very first word spoken on 'Emmerdale Farm' was Matt's name.

After that first episode, 'Emmerdale Farm' was broadcast at 1.30pm every Monday and Tuesday lunchtime and although the characters spoke with a strong but softened Yorkshire Dales accent, smattered occasionally with dialect terms, the dialogue was easily understood by the viewers. Director Gordon

Fleming had created real Yorkshire folk through his cast and true-to-life background. Initial viewing figures were 2,203,000.

From that first transmission, 'Emmerdale Farm' received high praise and a *Yorkshire Post* critic described it as, 'One of the most authentic rural series I have ever seen – it elevates the whole popular concept of country life.'

Jack did not particularly want the run-down farm and was quite happy that it should go to Peggy, but the terms of the will meant that it could not be done. Consequently, the ill-feeling between Jack and his family simmered dangerously but Jacob's will had achieved one objective – it had brought Jack home to Emmerdale. But not for long!

The pace of the story began to increase. In February 1973 Matt's wife, Peggy, gave birth to twins, a boy and a girl, Sam and Sally (who were played by the real-life twins of a family from Batley), and they went to live at Hawthorn Cottage, close to the farm. In March 1973 viewers saw the first Beckindale wedding. This was the marriage of Janie Harker (played by Diane Grayson) to the village blacksmith, Frank Blakey (played by Eric Allan). The ceremony was at St Mary's Parish Church, Beckindale, the best man was Jack Sugden and Joe was a guest. The officiating vicar was the Rev. Edward

Members of the cast of 'Emmerdale Farm' cutting the cake during the 10th anniversary celebrations in 1982. Back row, left to right: Ronald Magill, Arthur Pentelow, Clive Hornby; middle row: Fred Pyne, Jean Rogers (Dolly), Sheila Mercier, Helen Weir (Pat); seated: the late Toke Townley.

Ruskin. He was played by George Little and it was said that Mr Little looked more like a real vicar than most real vicars!

By April of the same year, only six months after its début, 'Emmerdale Farm' was shown on Yorkshire Television and Tyne-Tees TV as an hour-long edition beginning at 10.30pm after 'News at Ten'.

This comprised repeats of the episodes under the title of 'The Early Days of Emmerdale Farm' and the lunchtime viewing continued with the up-to-date story. Viewing figures had now increased to 3,000,000.

In that short time, Andrew Burt, in the character of surly Jack, had become TV's first matinée idol; women viewers loved the dark, brooding gipsy appearance and the sullen, unpredictable nature of this young farmer. One of his early escapades was to be discovered seducing the squire's wife, following which he was horse-whipped by the angry Squire Verney. Jack carried the scar on his cheek for a long time afterwards.

But Andrew Burt wanted to leave the serial to gain more acting experience. To accommodate his wishes, Jack was written out of the story. Jack was the author of a searing novel of life in the Dales, *Field of Tares*, and it had become a bestseller, so in January 1974 he went to live in Rome to work on a film script of his book.

Women everywhere were heartbroken at his departure but the impact of 'Emmerdale Farm' was maintained when a new charmer and a triple tragedy came into the story.

The charmer was a romantic gipsy character called Roy Boyd; he was discovered camping on Emmerdale land, and his dark long hair and bearded good looks concealed a roguish personality. None the less, he quickly made a few feminine hearts flutter before he moved on to continue his nomadic life.

The triple tragedy was to involve the quiet Matt Skilbeck and his young family. The first devastating blow to Matt and the Sugdens was when Matt's wife, Peggy, died suddenly. She had suffered from aneurysm, the rupture of a small artery in the brain, which had followed quickly after the birth of her twins, Sam and Sally. Her untimely death had struck so soon after Jacob Sugden's funeral. Matt, himself an orphan, had the difficult task of bringing up his little family single-handed while coping with the long, difficult and irregular hours of farm work, and so, to help him, Matt's Aunty Beatrice and Uncle Ben offered to care for the twins. They seemed ideal because Aunt Beatrice had once been a children's nanny, but soon there was even more devastating news – the twins and Aunt Beatrice were killed in a dreadful car crash. Matt was alone – and his role on the farm was uncertain; after all, he was not even a blood relation of the Sugdens, merely a farm employee. Annie, however, regarded Matt as a son and a very important part of her family, and so he remained at Emmerdale Farm to work it with Joe. Annie was a tower of strength as Matt tried to cope; she assumed the role of Matt's own mother as she helped him to overcome the trauma of his lost family.

'Emmerdale Farm' was continuing to receive flattering notices. The *Yorkshire Post* said, 'Afternoon viewing is becoming a "must" for a multitude of viewers, especially YTV's "Emmerdale Farm". It captures that elusive mixture of tranquillity and realism which is the essence of country life.'

Meanwhile, young and impressionable, Joe had fallen head over heels in

love with, and then married, the pretty dark-haired Christine Sharp (played by Angela Cheyne). They lived at their new home, Demdyke Cottage, and Christine worked for the Milk Marketing Board. She was not a Dales girl; as time went by, she came to realise that she could not tolerate the style of life offered at Beckindale; besides, her father had always been against her marriage.

He considered that Joe, as a farm labourer, was not good enough for his daughter and, no doubt aided by pressure from her father, Christine left Joe to consider her future. And she never returned. Joe would not leave Beckindale and so he and Christine were divorced. It was the first of many unfulfilled romances for Joe, and these helped him gain the sympathy and love of many ardent fans and viewers.

Peter Holman acted as producer for a few months, and under a new producer, a Californian called Robert D. Cardona, 'Emmerdale Farm' was attracting a wider audience because it was now being shown on most ITV regions at lunchtime, although at that time (1975), it had a summer break. Each year's transmission formed a new series of 'Emmerdale Farm', with long breaks during the summer and shorter ones in the winter, showing a total of twenty-six episodes each year. At this stage it was showing at 5.20pm on Yorkshire TV and Tyne-Tees TV and this resulted in complaints from some viewers because it clashed with tea-time and broke into children's viewing time.

A happy scene showing Matt with his twins, Sally and Sam, before they were tragically killed in a traffic accident at a railway level crossing.

The production team of 'Emmerdale Farm' enjoy visiting outside locations for recording – here at York Races, Joe shows a very young Jackie (Ian Sharrock) something of the mysteries of betting.

A change to the cast came with the departure of George Little who played the Rev. Edward Ruskin, and the arrival of a new lady character – Norah Norris the village shopkeeper (played by Barbara Ashcroft).

A new screening time was arranged, and in August 1976, after the summer break, the new series of 'Emmerdale Farm' appeared in many ITV regions at 3.50pm every weekday; these were selected repeats of the earlier episodes, and by November the same year this had settled down to two days a week, Mondays and Thursdays, on ITV regions. But more changes were on the way. By November 1976 'Emmerdale Farm' was screened at 3.50pm each Monday and Thursday on ITV regions, then during that winter and the following spring, several interesting new characters were introduced following the appointment of Michael Glynn as producer. Michael had previously worked with the BBC on live editions of the early 'Z-Cars' and as associate producer of 'Sutherland's Law' and 'The Troubleshooters', the latter taking him all over the world. His other work included 'The Borderers' and 'The Venturers', a story of merchant bankers, and he produced the second series of 'The Lotus Eaters'.

Michael wanted to work with 'Emmerdale Farm' not only because of its challenge as a twice-weekly serial, but also for its appeal as a family programme, which portrayed the tight family relationship that existed among the Sugdens.

He saw Annie as a strong mother character who sorted out her own problems as well as those of her family and indeed those of the village people who sought her advice. He felt that this picture of family life set against the beautiful countryside of the Yorkshire Dales offered wonderful opportunities for strong drama. Michael Glynn decided to make wider use of the countryside and outside broadcast cameras, to introduce more characters, some of whom would not be permanent, and to give more depth to the existing characters.

One of his early strands within the continuing story involved fell racing, a sport which is popular in the higher Dales. Joe Sugden was to participate in such a race and so the production team attended a real race meeting at Kilnsey Crag where actor Frazer Hines had to run with the actual competitors. He didn't beat them – but his efforts did bring more than a hint of realism to the programme.

Michael Glynn wanted to feature events which were taking place in the Dales, and one popular example was a story about a beautiful Swedish girl called Asta Gunnarson (played by Madeline Hinde), and her brother Olof (played by Jurgen Anderson); they had arrived in Beckindale to go pot-holing in the Dales. Very soon they were involved in a pot-hole rescue. Asta was trapped in Tom Taylor's Cave and the story featured the Wharfedale Cave Rescue Team of which Matt Skilbeck was a member.

This was a fine example of making use of the dramatic countryside which surrounded the fictitious Beckindale. It was also a tribute to the fact that 'Emmerdale Farm' was being viewed in Scandinavia where it was especially popular in Sweden. As part of Michael Glynn's determination to show more Yorkshire culture and heritage, he introduced strands in the story such as a pensioners' outing to Temple Newsham House near Leeds to visit the Museum. In that sequence Grandad Sam Pearson and the ladies of Beckindale had a day looking at the pictures and other exhibits, an experience shared by the viewers. Another innovation was to make 'Emmerdale Farm' seem more realistic by the introduction of some real-life topicality. This was achieved, for example, by having the people of Beckindale celebrate the Queen's Jubilee in 1977 by having a street party.

A topical note was introduced to 'Emmerdale Farm' in 1977 with the Silver Jubilee celebrations for HM The Queen. A street party was held in Beckindale and it was joined by all the cast, crew and villagers.

Around this time Grandad was temporarily written out of the story – he had apparently gone to Rome to work with Jack Sugden on a book about Sam Pearson's life, and the Woolpack got a new barmaid. She came from Darlington in County Durham. She was played by Katherine Barker, and Amos, who was initially wary of the pretty girl, pompously addressed her as Miss Acaster. Her name was Dolly – and she had a dark secret. Soon she was to fall in love with, and then marry, the widower Matt Skilbeck, although Matt did have another romance before he finally won Dolly. And Amos lost his reserve too – he grew to like the attractive and pleasant Dolly.

Lucy Stubbs (played by Adrienne Frank), was appointed as a trainee agricultural advisory officer at Hotten Mart with ADAS (the Agricultural Development and Advisory Service); she and Matt embarked on a brief romance before Matt married Dolly.

A new vicar came to Beckindale; he was the Rev. William Hockley (played by Jonathan Newth), but he was not to stay long. And even Henry Wilks found romance after a gap of some thirty years. On a visit to a near-by Dales village called Littlewell, he bumped into an old girlfriend, Janet Thompson (played by Muriel Pavlow), and they realised that the love they had borne for each other all those years ago had never died. The people of Beckindale – and many viewers – grew excited about a possible romance for Henry Wilks, the man who was such a benefactor to their community, but it did not flourish.

Meanwhile, Joe Sugden was recovering from a broken marriage. He found some consolation in a romance with local farmer's daughter Kathy Gimbel, whom he had known for a long time; she was also suffering from a broken marriage and eventually they decided to live together at Demdyke Cottage, an action which greatly displeased members of both families, especially Grandad Pearson. His views on morality were of the old-fashioned kind and he did not agree with Joe's actions – and he made his views known to his grandson. They were both still married to their other partners, for their divorces had not been finalised, and this ill-fated romance preceded the suicide of Kathy's father, Jim Gimbel.

As the story progressed and the characters developed, Michael Glynn appreciated just how successful Kevin Laffan's concept had become; the central characters perfectly symbolised the mainstays of traditional family life. Viewers could, and in fact did, easily identify with them. One interesting aspect was that the programme was often complimented for its refusal to use bad language, for its lack of innuendoes and its superb scenery with its clean air and gentle atmosphere. It was, in many ways, a portrayal of a very satisfying and desirable way of life.

'Emmerdale Farm's' rising popularity and its increasing number of viewers meant that in April 1977 it was transmitted at 7pm on Tuesdays and Thursdays on Yorkshire TV, Tyne-Tees TV and Border TV, with the other ITV regions broadcasting it during the mid-afternoon. But by the following August, ATV, Southern and Ulster TV screened it at the more important time of 7pm on Tuesdays and Thursdays, with Granada and Harlech showing it at 6.30pm on Tuesdays and Fridays, with the remaining ITV regions screening it at 5.15pm on Tuesdays and Thursdays. In Scotland, it was shown at 7pm on Tuesdays and Fridays.

This nationwide showing at prime viewing times was a massive upgrading for 'Emmerdale Farm' and it broadly remained in those slots until the spring of 1988 when it altered to 6.30pm on Wednesdays and Thursdays in all ITV regions, with viewing figures of around 11,000,000 in the United Kingdom. Viewing figures in 1977 were around 10 million, and the success of 'Emmerdale Farm' meant that in about five years it had moved from very localised lunchtime viewing through a mid-afternoon slot to peak-time viewing. This coincided with a necessary move from Arncliffe, the Dales village first used as the setting for Beckindale. It was too far from the studios, and the necessary travelling for location work was time-consuming and expensive. In those early days, the cast and crew had to stay overnight at local hotels and although Arncliffe was such a delightful setting, a new village had to be found for economic and practical reasons. That new village, which Yorkshire TV is contracted not to name, was selected with infinite care and it is still being used.

A temporary vicar came to Beckindale; he was the Rev. David Cowper (played by John Abbot), but he was soon replaced by the respected figure of the Rev. Donald Hinton (played by Hugh Manning).

Hinton was a man who so loved Beckindale and its people that he later refused the post of archdeacon when it was offered to him by the bishop.

During that 1977 series, Emmerdale Farm gave temporary shelter to an

The Dales village of Arncliffe has been described as 'a jewel between the wooded slopes of the moors and fells; it would be difficult to imagine a lovelier setting.'

Arncliffe was the first village to be used as the fictitious Beckindale, but its distance from the studios in Leeds meant that a new location had to be found. Arncliffe ended its TV role as Beckindale in 1977.

unemployed man called Ray and his wife Sarah who was nine months pregnant; their own cottage had been damaged when a tree was felled by lightning. The farm also took in Angela, a difficult child from a broken home who came to stay with the Sugdens through a scheme sponsored by the church. Angela was played by sixteen-year-old Joanne Whalley.

At this time Amos Brearly was making his name as the Beckindale correspondent to the *Hotten Courier*, a newspaper introduced to the serial by Michael Glynn, and Joe became an auxiliary fireman to be later reunited with an old flame called Lesley Gibson (played by Jane Collins).

In June 1979 'Emmerdale Farm's' first woman producer joined the programme; she was Anne W. Gibbons and she introduced several new faces to the cast. She felt that the strength of 'Emmerdale Farm' lay in the serial element rather than a succession of shorter stories involving characters who were brought in temporarily. She required a greater number of permanent characters about whom strong stories could be woven. She introduced Seth Armstrong as a permanent character rather than one who popped in and out of stories; she introduced the Merricks who later had to cope with Sandie's pregnancy, the true identity of Jackie's father, the burning of Jackie's caravan and a whole new range of stories surrounding Tom and Pat Merrick and their family.

Anne Gibbons also caused Joe to leave Emmerdale Farm in favour of a career with NY Estates and she was also to introduce Alan Turner to viewers and then baby Sam Skilbeck, named in honour of Sam Pearson.

But Jack Sugden, having fulfilled his wish to earn a living away from Emmerdale Farm, returned permanently to the village and so Anne Gibbons introduced us to yet another new face. Clive Hornby was the actor who played the more mature Jack, and he came back to Emmerdale because he loved his roots, the Yorkshire countryside and the life-style of his heritage. For a while, he did not work on the farm but adopted a Bohemian way of life and lived alone in an old mill near the farm. But in time, he settled down to bring Emmerdale into the twentieth century, and was helped by Henry Wilks who

Below: *In his younger days, Joe Sugden became a very enthusiastic member of the auxiliary Fire Brigade.*

Henry Wilks with a peregrine falcon used for falconry.

had injected some much-needed cash into the farm. Henry then became a partner in Emmerdale Farm Ltd but some of his business ideas did not suit Jack's view of the traditional method of farming. Jack was to find some of Henry's views very restrictive – but the farm did now have some security.

A second actress was also appointed to play Dolly Acaster and her name was Jean Rogers. She was to prove a delight in this part, especially when Dolly married the slow-moving, steady Matt Skilbeck after some momentary indecision when her former lover arrived on the scene.

Jean has always played the loving wife, a picture of charm and patience, who was tolerant of Matt's lack of ambition, but who secretly wanted to move away from Emmerdale to have a home of her own and who yearned for a more exciting life. But the return of Jack and the marriage of Matt and Dolly put enormous pressure on the limited accommodation in the farm house, and so Anne Gibbons supervised the conversion of a barn into a new home for Matt and Dolly. They loved their delightful cottage which adjoined the farm, but Dolly's dream of a place of her own was to result in some future high drama. In 1988 the deserted farm house known as Crossgill was left to Dolly

A happy family snapshot of the Skilbecks. Matt and Dolly with baby Sam (Benjamin Whitehead).

37

Joint Pipemen of the Year, 1986, Amos Brearly and Henry Wilks.

and Matt in a will. It needed lots of renovation but it was Dolly's dream home ... until it burned down. And then she fell in love with the handsome and rakish Stephen Fuller....

But much earlier, Dolly's happiness had seemed complete because she became a mother for the second time; her first child, fathered by her former lover, had been born before her marriage and had been adopted, but in 1983 she gave birth to a son. The christening of Samuel David Skilbeck took place in St Mary's Parish Church, Beckindale, when he was four and half months old.

The recording of this event took place during the 800th episode of 'Emmerdale Farm' and it was transmitted on 6 May 1983, and Sam started school on 17 September 1987, the day Jack Sugden was released from prison after his protest over the threatened disposal of nuclear waste near Beckindale.

38

Long before this incident, however, Jack Sugden, following his return from Rome, had been busy renewing his acquaintance with a past girlfriend. She was the former Pat Harker who was now Mrs Pat Merrick, the victim of an unhappy marriage and the mother of two teenagers, Sandie and Jackie, both growing fast. But the viewer (and most of Beckindale!) was to learn that Jackie was not the natural son of Tom Merrick. His real father was Jack Sugden. But the lad had been brought up by Merrick in the full belief that he was the father; in spite of his rough character, his skirmishes with the law and his general inability to hold down a steady job, Merrick did love his children and his wife. But he beat her from time to time and she led a miserable life, eventually leaving him to live in a rented caravan in Beckindale. The children moved in with her and it was from this point that Pat Merrick renewed her romance with Jack Sugden, a romance which led to a fight outside the Woolpack between Jack and Tom Merrick.

But this did not deter Jack and Pat, for they were married in Hotten Registrar's Office in the face of considerable hostility from Jackie.

This hatred of Jack was almost to destroy young Jackie's future, for he turned to drink and rebellious behaviour – but Annie helped him come to terms with his 'new' father.

With the 800th episode behind them, it was discovered that the teenage Sandie Merrick (played by Jane Hutcheson) was pregnant.

She received sympathetic help from Dolly Skilbeck in her first uncertain months, but steadfastly refused to name the father – it later transpired that he was Andy Longthorn, son of a local farmer and a former schoolmate of Sandie's. Andy had gone to University, and to avoid shaming her mother, Sandie went to Aberdeen to have her baby. She lived with her father in a flat; he had secured a well-paid job with an oil rig and after some time off-shore, was given a shore job. For the first time in his life Tom Merrick seemed to be settling down and Sandie found that he was a tremendous support during her pregnancy. When Sandie's daughter was born, she had the child adopted, a sad decision, and for a long time she was angry and upset that her mother had not come to visit her, especially during her confinement and birth. Her resentment kept her away from her mother but in time she returned to Emmerdale, at first for a short break with her father who claimed he had some business to settle in Hotten, and finally as a member of the family at Emmerdale Farm where she and Grandad Pearson struck up a firm friendship.

Sandie's change of heart resulted from several factors; one was that her father, when visiting Hotten, had returned to his old ways. Having embarked upon an unsuccessful poaching trip, he was arrested and sent to prison; worse still, he had persuaded Jackie to go with him. Jackie, fortunately, had had the sense to return home once he discovered the truth of his 'father's' late-night excursion and so he was not prosecuted.

But Sandie's real reason for returning was because she had become reconciled with her mother – this had come about through several factors. There had been an upheaval in her life when she discovered that Jackie was not her full brother, and this revelation was made worse because the father was Jack Sugden. But Sandie was intelligent and adaptable; she had a deep desire to make a success of her life and as a schoolgirl had nursed an ambition to secure

Sandie Merrick (Jane Hutcheson) is about to discover the truth about her boss, Eric Pollard (Christopher Chittell).

'A' levels and go to Warwick University to read Physics. She did not achieve those aims, but did succeed admirably in picking up the threads of her shaken life by obtaining a job at Hotten Mart where she decided to study as an auctioneer. She passed her exams, but in the meantime Phil Pearce, married with a child, had come into her life. She fell in love with him but her earlier experiences had taught her the need for caution. Phil obtained a divorce and together they set up home in an old converted mill at Connelton. Then Sandie caught her auctioneer boss Eric Pollard fiddling the books of the auctioneer's office at Hotten Mart, and he was sacked.

Sandie secured the job and with it the hatred and envy of Pollard, but it wasn't long before her job vanished when NY Estates closed their Beckindale operation and the Hotten Mart was shut down. She became pregnant again but lost the baby due to a miscarriage and then found she did not love Phil. In 1988 salvation came when Hotten Mart was purchased by the council who re-opened it to present her with a new opportunity in her career as an auctioneer.

Anne Gibbons concluded her spell as producer in June 1983, and the responsibility passed to Richard Handford. By this time the saga of this pretty Yorkshire village was attracting interest across the world, and in 1983 two series of 'Emmerdale Farm' were brought by a TV company in the Arab Republic of Egypt.

If 1983 led to a drastic change in Sandie's life, it also affected her brother, Jackie. A minor character in the series since 1980, Jackie (played by Ian Sharrock), was now to feature strongly in the story. With Jack as his natural father, he was the heir to Emmerdale Farm but this did not immediately impress him; a tempestuous youth, his initial reaction was that both he and his mother had been rejected by Jack, and he could not see that their new love affair made any difference. He became a very awkward and difficult lad who was in constant trouble with the police but who did try to understand game-keeping when he worked for NY Estates. Seth taught him as best he could and formed a close friendship with his young trainee but Jackie's ambition was to join the Army and gain some excitement as a parachutist. But Jackie made a mess of organising a shooting party for NY Estates and Alan Turner sacked him, excusing his decision by saying it was a cost-saving necessity.

Alan Turner (Richard Thorp) tries to sort out a problem with his work force.

And Jackie, who was living in a caravan rented by his mother from NY Estates because he could not tolerate being under the same roof as Jack Sugden, set fire to the caravan in a fit of revenge. He was prosecuted and sentenced to a period of community service.

His conviction ruined his chance of a career in the Army and he had no choice but to settle down to life at Emmerdale Farm; but there was more strife. He was later knocked down by Alan Turner's Land-Rover and placed in hospital with serious injuries. In his agony and distress his new family rallied around and he began to appreciate the worth of real love and a real family life; he began to show a keen interest in the work at Emmerdale, at first being far from co-operative with Jack. But Jack won him over; soon, young Jackie was thriving as he found himself busy assisting Matt, helping around the farm, learning the skills and finding delight in the new lambs and the art of training a sheepdog . . . a new and mature Jackie emerged, one who is now a credit to Emmerdale and who has a whole new life ahead since his marriage to Kathy Bates.

Seth Armstrong was having marriage problems too; his long-suffering wife, Meg, threatened to throw him out if he did not drink less. Seth obstinately refused and Meg did throw him out; he then had to sleep rough but eventually he wheedled his way back into the house. Meg was originally played by Ursula Camm but her part is now taken by Ruth Holden; her appearances are rare,

When Jackie Merrick was injured in an accident with Alan Turner's Landrover, he received first-class treatment from the police and ambulance services.

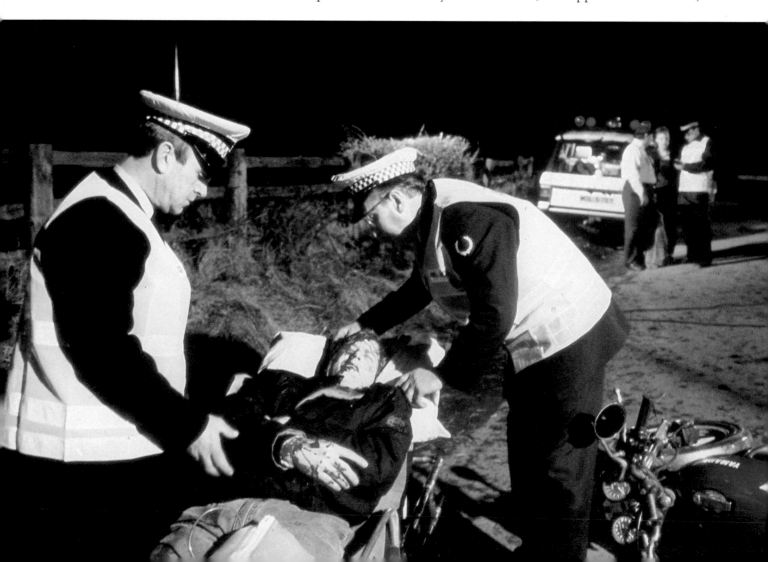

although for a time she did help behind the bar of the Woolpack where she could keep an eye on Seth's drinking!

More romance came to Joe in the shape of an attractive girl called Barbara Peters (played by Rosie Kerslake), and upon first meeting her, Joe got very upset when he found she was staying overnight with the vicar. . . .

When he later discovered she was the Rev. Hinton's daughter, he was most relieved – and very interested. But Barbara had problems too. She had abandoned her husband, and so the vicar was suffering the turmoil of a conflict between his faith and his daughter's delicate situation of being a married woman who was seeing another man – Joe Sugden! Barbara worked for a time as Alan Turner's secretary at NY Estates.

This love match caused intense interest among the viewers, but it was evident to them (if not to Joe) that Barbara was going to leave Beckindale. This caused widespread speculation that Joe's anguish, when Barbara eventually left him, would cause the script-writers to make something awful happen to Joe, that he would be killed off, perhaps, or even commit suicide . . . some of the very anxious fans protested at these possibilities when it became known that Frazer Hines wished to leave 'Emmerdale Farm' for a period of assessment of his own life.

These speculations coincided with the 10th anniversary of 'Emmerdale Farm' and Joe did leave the programme in 1983. This was reflected in the story by having Joe feeling very upset at Barbara's apparent rejection of him, but also that there was no future for him with NY Estates. And so Joe Sugden went to France where he was employed by NY Estates in their French office near Tours; his mother missed him dearly.

With Joe out of the programme, feminine interest was now concentrated

Above left: *Seth Armstrong is always one for bending the rules, and when the Woolpack Inn ran a competition for the best bunch of daffodils, Seth reckoned those growing at Home Farm were winners. But Nick Bates (Cy Chadwick) caught him in the act of picking his 'show' entry . . .*

Above right: *Joe's romance with the married daughter of the Rev Donald Hinton, Mrs Barbara Peters (Rosie Kerslake), caused heartache for the vicar, but it was an ill-fated love story. Barbara left Joe to continue her life without him, so he obtained a post with NY Estates in France.*

43

upon Jackie Merrick, Jack's natural son who was struggling to come to terms with his future role as the heir to Emmerdale Farm. He was still getting into scrapes with the law and having a series of unfulfilled love affairs with some nice girls, and some very unsuitable ones. But Jackie was growing up very quickly, and his maturity occurred one night when Jack, Pat, Matt and Dolly were out at dinner; a cow began to give birth to a calf and Jackie had to cope.

He did so by recruiting the help of the vicar and Henry Wilks who were dining with Annie at Emmerdale. This gave Jackie enormous pride and self-confidence, so much so that he settled down to the farming and his new responsibilities. He worked cheerfully alongside his true father and his mother who was herself struggling to understand the many aspects of farming.

Meanwhile, at NY Estates, Alan Turner, the estates manager who had followed David Thatcher, Bruce Westrop and Richard Anstey into the difficult job of making NY Estates' venture in Beckindale both viable and profitable, was having problems. Head Office was demanding further economies of both finances and staff; there was talk of redundancies and as the major employer in Beckindale, Alan Turner knew this could create hardship in the community.

As he struggled to retain his work force, he took to gambling and drink.

Overwork, through lack of a secretary, was also making the situation worse – several part-time secretaries had come and gone for few could tolerate Turner's excesses, and one left following his clumsy attempt to seduce her in the Woolpack Inn. His antics caused hilarity throughout the village, but Annie came to his rescue. She secretly recruited the help of Turner's estranged wife, Jill, who ran a thriving business in Manchester, and so he was helped to re-establish himself and to regain his self-respect. Then Head Office relented over his requests for a secretary and he was allowed to recruit a very efficient lady, provided she had computer skills and could operate a word processor. And so Mrs Caroline Bates, with a daughter called Kathy and a son called Nick, came to Beckindale. She was having domestic problems too, for her husband, Malcolm, a freelance lecturer, had found a younger woman. . . .

But more real drama was to follow in 1984. A devastating blow to the serial was the death of Toke Townley who played Grandad Sam Pearson. Taken ill during a shopping trip, Toke was admitted to hospital for forty-eight hours' observation, but died suddenly during the night. The script writers had hurriedly to write in the death of Sam, and in the story Annie took her father his morning cup of tea in bed and found he had peacefully faded away in his sleep. Both Grandad and Toke are sadly missed.

Another strong piece of fiction occurred in the winter of 1986, when the placid and unshakeable Matt Skilbeck found himself suspected of murder. Long before this, there had been bad feeling between Matt and Harry Mowlem, a local quarry owner, due to Mowlem's cruel treatment of his dog, Ben. Matt took the dog home and refused to allow Mowlem to have it back and the antagonism increased when Mowlem accused Matt of stealing the dog . . . then Matt and Mowlem had a stand-up fight beside the brook in Beckindale and the normally placid Matt thrashed the ill-loved Mowlem.

Next morning Henry Wilks, out for a morning walk, came across Mowlem's body in the stream and even Matt wondered if he had caused the fellow's death. Matt was arrested – and viewing figures increased as the popular press

When Matt lost his temper with Harry Mowlem (Godfrey James), it led to a charge of murder being preferred against Matt – and even Matt wasn't sure whether he had killed Mowlem.

During a morning walk, Henry Wilks finds the body of Harry Mowlem.

speculated whether the calm and tolerant Matt could stir himself to kill another human being. Even the police in Manchester were placing bets as to whether or not Matt was guilty, half of them believing he was and half believing in his innocence! Later it transpired that Mowlem had been involved in some cash robberies with Derek Warner, one of Tom Merrick's less savoury friends and it was Warner who had killed Mowlem in an argument about the share-out of the stolen money. Matt was exonerated, but not before Dolly had experienced the chill of the reaction from her so-called friends when Matt's innocence was very much in doubt.

And all the time, there were hints of a romance between the objectionable Alan Turner and his patient secretary, Mrs Bates, but nothing has ever happened and viewers are still wondering when they will become romantically involved. . . .

Meanwhile, Kathy Bates was maturing into a lovely and bubbly blonde young woman, but Joe Sugden could not stay away from his beloved Beckindale. He returned in 1986, ostensibly for a holiday but he had discovered that the job of Regional Manager of NY Estates was being advertised. Turner had applied – and so Joe also made application.

To the surprise and delight of his family and indeed the whole of Beckindale, Joe was appointed, thus becoming boss of his previous boss and making a welcome return to Beckindale and to Emmerdale Farm. For a time, there was just a hint of a romance between the mature Joe and the youthful Kathy who is played by Malandra Burrows. This romance did not proceed, but his brother, Jack, did stray by having an affair with Karen Moore (played by Annie Hulley); she was a secretary at Hotten Mart and very soon Jack was involved in a steamy and passionate relationship with her. This story was introduced by Richard Handford who, like Anne Gibbons, felt the saga of 'Emmerdale Farm' should strongly involve the main characters rather than make use of satellite characters who flitted in and out of the serial.

And so to maintain the dramatic impact and to inject more drama into the lives of the Sugdens, Jack found himself pitched headlong into a highly charged love affair.

It caused a storm among the viewers who felt this kind of story was not in keeping with 'Emmerdale Farm', but viewing figures soared, so much so that 'Emmerdale Farm' leapt into the top ten of the JICTAR ratings (Joint Industry Committee for Television Advertising Research), and at one stage was third in the top twenty ratings of both BBC and ITV dramas.

The end came when Karen wanted Jack to leave Pat – what had started as a casual friendship and then a romance had now developed into a full-blooded love affair. But Pat discovered Jack's secret and confronted them at Karen's flat. Calmly, she gave Jack an ultimatum – either he left Karen immediately to return to Emmerdale, or he would never see Pat again. Jack made his decision – he returned to Pat.

The production team felt that their treatment of this story strand was one of their best, and it had certainly made an impact on the viewers as well as leading to an increase in the audience figures. Afterwards Jack made a very determined effort to salvage his marriage and it was followed by the happy news that Pat, already with grown-up children, was pregnant. Jack and Pat

were delighted and were loving parents to the new-born Robert when he arrived.

Karen was low in the estimation of the people of Beckindale because she also had an affair with Joe, but in real life, actor Clive Hornby (Jack) and his wife, Helen Weir (Pat), were having their own child.

And when their son was born, Helen realised she wanted to spend more time at home with him. This presented a problem for producer Richard Handford – how could Pat Sugden, mother and wife, be written out of the serial? The answer came with yet more controversial drama. There was an horrific car crash when Pat swerved on a Dales road to avoid a flock of sheep, and she died leaving a son of a few months, and 'Emmerdale Farm' viewers shared Jack's utter misery in some superb acting by Clive Hornby. That was Richard Handford's parting highspot and so Jack was left with a tiny son called Robert. He was a baby brother for the maturing Jackie and a new grandchild for Annie. What kind of future lay ahead for Jack and his infant son?

The task of producing the scenes which involved Pat's funeral in August 1986, fell to a new producer, Michael Russell. He had been with 'Emmerdale Farm' since 1978, working as script editor (1978–81), script consultant (1981–3) and as a writer before becoming the new producer. Pat's death is commemorated in an epitaph on her gravestone which reads 'Patricia Sugden, died 26th August, 1986. Rest in Peace', followed by a quotation from Bishop Henry King (1592–1669):

> But hark! My pulse like a soft drum
> Beats my approach, tells thee I come;
> And slow howe'er my marches be
> I shall at last sit down by thee.

But another character entered the serial – Phil Pearce, an old friend of Joe's who had returned to re-establish himself at Hotten as a builder. Phil was

Above left: Joe Sugden takes up his new appointment as Regional Manager for NY Estates upon his return from France. He is seen here with Alan Turner.

Above right: Friends and family at Beckindale Parish Church following the christening of Robert Sugden (Richard Smith), son of Jack and the late Pat Sugden.

married to Lesley (played by Clare Clifford), and they had a young daughter, but it wasn't long before Phil found himself attracted to Sandie Merrick.

Phil (played by Peter Alexander), is a weak and somewhat feckless person whose business enterprises are not always successful or practicable, but he won Sandie's heart. Phil set up a construction business with Joe, one of their projects being to renovate an old mill at Connelton, which was to become home for Phil and Sandie. Meanwhile, Phil had abandoned his wife and child for Sandie, an act which caused Lesley Pearce to confront Sandie in the Woolpack with an accusation that she was a tart who had stolen her husband. For a time, Phil and Sandie lived with Joe in Demdyke Cottage before moving to their new home at the converted mill, but it was not long before Sandie began to realise that Phil was never totally dependable; a terrible example came in a near tragic episode when he left some rags to burn in Crossgill, the old farm house which was to become home for Matt and Dolly. He rescued Annie from the blaze, but in his heart he felt he had almost caused her death.

Poor Dolly had had another shock, too, the previous Christmas. A strange youth arrived in Beckindale; he was camping rough in the woods and even destroyed his own car.

This was Graham, Dolly's illegitimate son who was now eighteen and a soldier. He had come to find his true mother, the woman whom he thought had abandoned him as a baby and he told stirring stories of his life in the

Royal Navy. But in reality he was a deserter from the Army and was returned to camp by a Sergeant Major.

Michael Russell introduced a very topical storyline in 1987 when there were rumours that Pencross Fell was to be the site of an underground nuclear waste dump. In real life, this subject was causing public concern in rural areas and in the 'Emmerdale Farm' storyline Jack Sugden was both horrified and dismayed at this news. He did not wish his new son, his family or the people of Beckindale to live with the threat of nuclear waste so close to the village and the family farm. He fought hard against the proposals and organised a powerful protest which resulted in him serving a week in prison for contempt of court – and the plans were abandoned. Jack's lone protest had not really caused this change of heart, but in his mind it was more than a coincidence. This highly topical story brought to the public eye some of the issues associated with this very real problem. Some reaction from viewers said that the treatment of this story was politically too left wing and others felt it was too right wing, while many considered it not the kind of story that should be featured in 'Emmerdale Farm'.

Michael Russell said, 'In producing "Emmerdale Farm", we never preach about the issues which are presented – we tell the story and we let the viewers make their own judgements.'

And as we come to the more recent story of 'Emmerdale Farm', Jack has left the village and the farm to embark upon another of his ventures, while Joe is struggling with Alan Turner and Mrs Bates, to make a success of Home Farm Estate, once the home of the Verneys and, in recent years, the centre of NY Estates in Beckindale.

Joe has been enduring yet another ill-fated romance, this time with the

Below left: When Dolly's illegitimate son, Graham (Ross Kemp), arrived unexpectedly in Beckindale, it was not an easy time for either of them. Dolly had had Graham adopted at birth and he was seeking his true mother, a mother he had never known.

Below right: Archie (Tony Pitts) makes his own protest against the proposed dumping of nuclear waste on Pencross Fell.

Matt and Ian Sharrock tending a new-born lamb.

lovely veterinary surgeon Ruth Pennington (played by Julia Chambers) while Annie continues to be mother and friend of all – even though she has troubles of her own. Jackie and Kathy are settling into their marriage with no sign of a baby at this stage.

Seth Armstrong is continuing to bait Amos Brearly at the Woolpack Inn while Amos and Wilks run their pub on traditional lines; it remains the communications centre of Beckindale. If anything new is going to happen in Beckindale, the news will probably be told first in the famous bar of the Woolpack Inn.

Matt and Dolly are trying to come to terms with the awful series of events that has plagued their lives in recent months, while she and Kathy have a new interest, for they have opened a farm shop at Emmerdale. Each believes that a woman should have interests outside the home and the kitchen.

50

How they all cope will be among the many questions to be answered in this compelling story of Yorkshire Dalesfolk and the countryside in which they live and work. The drama will be seen by many nationalities, for 'Emmerdale Farm' is now viewed in countries as diverse as New Zealand, Swaziland, Sweden, Eire and Holland in addition to broadcasts on the new European Super Channel.

In 1987 'Emmerdale Farm' was the first British dramatic serial to appear on the new European Super Channel with viewers now numbering some 11,000,000 in the United Kingdom and millions more overseas.

Kevin Laffan, whose idea has created an entire 'Emmerdale Farm' industry, continues his interest as adviser and consultant to the serial, and in April 1988 'Emmerdale Farm' featured on the BBC TV series 'Open Air' – high praise indeed, especially since it came from the opposition.

Annie Sugden in discussion with her two sons, Jack (left) and Joe.

Before his marriage in 1988, Jackie Merrick had several romances. Here he is (clockwise from top left), in 1981 with Jane (Alison Dowling); 1983, with Maggie (Jacqueline Reddin); 1984, with Alison (Julie Brennon); and 1985, with Sita (Mamta Kash).

Chapter Three

The Production Process

Preparing the Scripts

Every development in the continuing story of 'Emmerdale Farm' begins with a script conference involving the producer, the story editor, the script editor and the team of ten script writers. Between them, they create the long-term storyline and a series of shorter stories or 'strands' which will feature within the main progression of the serial. Major developments of the story or the individual characters are discussed with the executive producer because the long-term story must evolve around the central characters and it must show a continuation of their lives with all the triumphs and problems that are involved.

From time to time other characters will enter the story, perhaps for a short period as they become involved with the people of Beckindale or the family at Emmerdale Farm, but these rarely become a permanent feature of the on-going story. From time to time, however, it is necessary to introduce a major new character or to lose one of the main characters in a manner which does become a permanent feature of the story. In this way real life is mirrored within the serial. Births, deaths, absences from home, interaction with other people and places are all aspects of normal life that must be shown at some time within 'Emmerdale Farm'.

As the various avenues of the story are explored, with the co-operation of the story editor, Andrew Holden, the producer will decide which will be featured on our screens and in making these decisions the permitted budget for the programme must be borne in mind, as must the use of the outdoor locations, the studio sets, the presence or absence of the cast and many other factors. The serial must be completed within the budget and time allowed.

When the long-term storyline has been decided, perhaps as much as a year in advance, writers will be commissioned. Each will write two half-hour episodes which is one hour's viewing time, bearing in mind the opening sequences, the mid-programme advertisements and the closing credits. The writers for 'Emmerdale Farm' are permitted considerable freedom in the preparation of their scripts, although they must follow the prepared storyline.

The script editor, David Lane, works closely with the writers, providing background information, help and advice and ensuring that continuity and characterisation are accurate.

When the scripts have been written, revised and edited, they are duplicated for circulation to a whole range of people involved in the production, including the executive producer, producer, director, script editor, production assistant, unit manager, stage manager, those responsible for casting, design, make-up, camera work, sound, vision, costume, carpenters, electricians, technical support and the supply of props.

Others in receipt of a copy include the accounts department, stills photography department (who are responsible for the range of superb illustrations in this book), regular writers, the script library and many others, including, of course, members of the cast. Their work involves learning the lines in the scripts so that a convincing performance is produced for the benefit of the viewers.

Rehearsal

When the story of 'Emmerdale Farm' appears on the TV screen, viewers are tempted to believe they are enjoying a privileged visit to real people who live and work in a genuine Yorkshire village. This blurring of the distinction between fact and fiction is one of the strengths of 'Emmerdale Farm', but the aura of realism is also a massive tribute to members of the cast. Their acting is so good that it convinces the viewers they are real Dales people.

This skill does not come easily; it requires hour after hour of very hard work and dogged determination by the artistes, the director and his production crew. Each seeks to reproduce exactly the right effect on screen and this can be achieved by something as small as a glance, a facial expression or tiny movement of the body. These visual messages are supported by words and action, but so much can be portrayed without a word being said – and it is here that the 'Emmerdale Farm' actors are so proficient.

But such acting skill is the outcome of hours of hard work away from the cameras and it is this which produces such compulsive and relaxed viewing. After reading the scripts and learning their lines, the artistes assemble in their rehearsal suite below the 'Emmerdale Farm' offices at Yorkshire Television's studios in Leeds.

As they await their calls to rehearse a particular scene, they relax in the Green Room, re-reading their lines, dealing with any mail that has arrived and discussing their work with fellow actors.

Every scene is then rehearsed and analysed, the artistes working with the production crew and director to point out any matter which might cause a problem when the scene is recorded. These could be something as basic as the time required for Annie to boil an egg or for Joe to walk across a room or for the family to eat a meal. In one sequence, actor Gregory Floy who played Dolly's illicit lover, Stephen Fuller, pointed out that Stephen had not met Annie before arriving at Emmerdale Farm for a meal; therefore introductions

Above: *A script conference with the 'Emmerdale Farm' writers. Producer Stuart Doughty sits at the head of the table (left) with story editor Andrew Holden at his side. Sitting apart in the top right corner is David Lane, the script editor.*

Centre: *A table in the rehearsal room becomes Annie Sugden's kitchen table. Note the markings on the floor (see page 56).*

Below: *The rehearsal room. Here, Stan Richards, Drew Dawson and Richard Thorp rehearse a scene in their own clothes. When transmitted, the scene will be Home Farm Estate Office, the table will be Turner's desk, and the characters will be Seth Armstrong, Jock MacDonald and Alan Turner, all dressed for their parts.*

*Short conferences
between members of the
production team are
regular events. Here, a
matter of interpretation
of the script is cleared up
and a lighting problem is
solved.*

had to be made, and so at rehearsal these were written into the script and
included in the finished scene. It was a vital point if realism was to be
maintained.

The rehearsal room is somewhat spartan in appearance, but it serves many
purposes.

The floor is marked with a web of coloured lines and if they first appear to
be meaningless, they are in fact the floor outlines of the rooms which appear
in 'Emmerdale Farm'. Also in the room is a selection of small tables, chairs,
settees, some large counters on wheels, crockery of all kinds and a host of
props which find themselves in use as the actors improvise during their
rehearsal. For example, by moving the chair, settees and a dining table into
one of the outlines on the floor, Annie's famous farm kitchen is represented;
by shifting the settee and chairs elsewhere, it becomes the living room in Dolly
and Matt's cottage or the back room of the Woolpack Inn. In another switch
of furniture, it can be the bar of the Woolpack Inn or the office at Home Farm.
Those large counters on wheels can serve as Annie's kitchen sink, a piano, the
bar at the Woolpack or the sideboard in Sandie's home. A baked-beans tin can
be anything from a can of beer to a champagne glass while an old rag may
serve as a makeshift tea-cloth, towel, piece of knitting or a clip rug being
worked by Annie. It is a very plain room which serves a highly important
function.

But in another part of the YTV complex the rooms known so well by the
viewers *can* be seen – but even these are not real. Annie's farm kitchen is not
in the farm house which is used for the outdoor scenes – it is in the studio at
Leeds, along with the bar of the Woolpack Inn, the interior of Matt and
Dolly's cottage and many other internal settings.

However, it is in the bare room with its multi-coloured floor that the vital
rehearsals continue, with production crew and artistes working together in a
most remarkable and friendly manner. These long days at rehearsal also serve

another purpose, for they are witnessed by other members of the team who are involved in the production process.

For example, the lighting director observes the scenes during a special lighting run so that he can decide upon the necessary lighting during shooting; he needs to know the positions of the actors, the props and the lights themselves, while the designer plots on sheets of paper the moves of the characters and the position of the furniture and props for the benefit of the cameras at a later stage. The stage manager and assistant stage manager call in the actors, arrange the scenery and act as prompters from the script, while the director supervises and guides the action. His task is to direct the artistes during their performance, calling for more emotion or less movement, positioning them in relation to the cameras and working to draw from them their very best performance even if this is a rehearsal.

It was during rehearsals that Jean Rogers as Dolly produced two powerful performances, one when she was trying to cope with the shock of losing Crossgill, the home upon which she had set her heart, and the second occurred after the handsome timber specialist Stephen Fuller had left after enjoying a brandy with herself and Matt.

A very familiar kitchen begins to take shape in the studio.

She lifted his glass from the mantelpiece ... and we all knew she was falling in love with him. Similarly, in one study of his face, Peter Alexander managed to convey all the agony that Phil Pearce felt when he realised he might, however accidentally, have caused the fire which destroyed Dolly's dream.

Because of their very nature, the necessary repetition and the enormous wealth of detail, including complex technical considerations that have to be checked over and over again, rehearsals are long and tiring, both for the artistes and the production crew. And while rehearsals by some artistes are in progress in the rehearsal room, other members of the cast will be in the studio or out on location recording the necessary scenes for the story. It is a relentless, tiring and difficult time, but vitally important.

Fortunately, in the case of 'Emmerdale Farm', this onerous task is tempered with good humour, friendliness and a remarkable rapport between everyone involved.

In the Studio

The atmosphere of 'Emmerdale Farm' is generated through a careful blending of outdoor scenes, which depict farm and village life in the picturesque countryside of the Yorkshire Dales, and an equally careful selection of indoor scenes through which the viewers observe events around the homes and workplaces of the characters.

It is easy to believe that Annie Sugden's famous kitchen is actually in the farm house which doubles as Emmerdale Farm, or that the bar of the Woolpack Inn is within the building used as the 'superior hostelry' so beloved by Amos Brearly. To this list can be added the interior of other places which are so familiar to the viewers such as the office of the former NY Estates, now Home Farm Estates, the back room of the Woolpack Inn, the kitchen and lounge of Mrs Bates's cottage, the interior of Matt and Dolly's home which adjoins Emmerdale Farm or indeed the settings for most of the interior scenes.

It comes as something of a surprise or even a shock to learn that, almost without exception, these interiors are nothing more than studio creations. They are nowhere near the outdoor locations which are so familiar as the background to Emmerdale Farm, but are neatly packed away in storerooms to be built when required in the studio at Yorkshire Television in Leeds.

These realistic sets are built by experts to serve a purpose similar to the scenery in a theatre. The sturdy panelled walls of Home Farm Office in its splendid setting on a country estate are, in reality, nothing more than fabricated hardboard and wooden copies which, when not in use, await their turn in a YTV storeroom. Walls can be added as required; it takes but a few minutes for an extra wall, which is already prepared for such eventuality, to be included if needed. Added to this, there is the furniture, the various ornaments, carpets, kitchen utensils or other fittings and all the complementary items which serve to add that vital touch of realism to any of the sets.

Who is not familiar with the bar of the Woolpack Inn or Annie Sugden's farm-house kitchen? It takes about an hour for such a set to be built to a pre-

arranged plan – even the enormous fireplace in the Woolpack looks genuine as does the entire appearance of Annie's kitchen, and this applies to all the sets which many viewers accept as being so real.

The key to the magic of this necessary deception lies in Studio 3, deep within the Yorkshire TV complex at Leeds. It is a massive room reminiscent of an aircraft hangar and it has a lofty ceiling which is invisible above an incredibly complex assortment of lighting, air-conditiong plant, technical equipment and the other paraphernalia of a television production. Huge lights hang from retractable stems, some of which are in use while others await their turn.

The floor of Studio 3 is about the size of two full-size tennis courts and the interior is sound-proofed so that no external noise filters in during recording. High on one wall is a sound-proofed glass window and behind this is the control room; access to the control room from the studio floor is via a long, steep and narrow flight of steps which clings to the wall like a ship's ladder hugging its parent hulk. At the top of that staircase are other offices and rooms, the whole of which is known as the Gallery.

By standing in the control room it is possible to peer into the depths of Studio 3 but the real contact with the army of people who form the cast and production crew is done through microphones, headsets and various internal communication systems. It is the presence of so much technical equipment

EMMERDALE FARM IN STUDIO AT YORKSHIRE TELEVISION

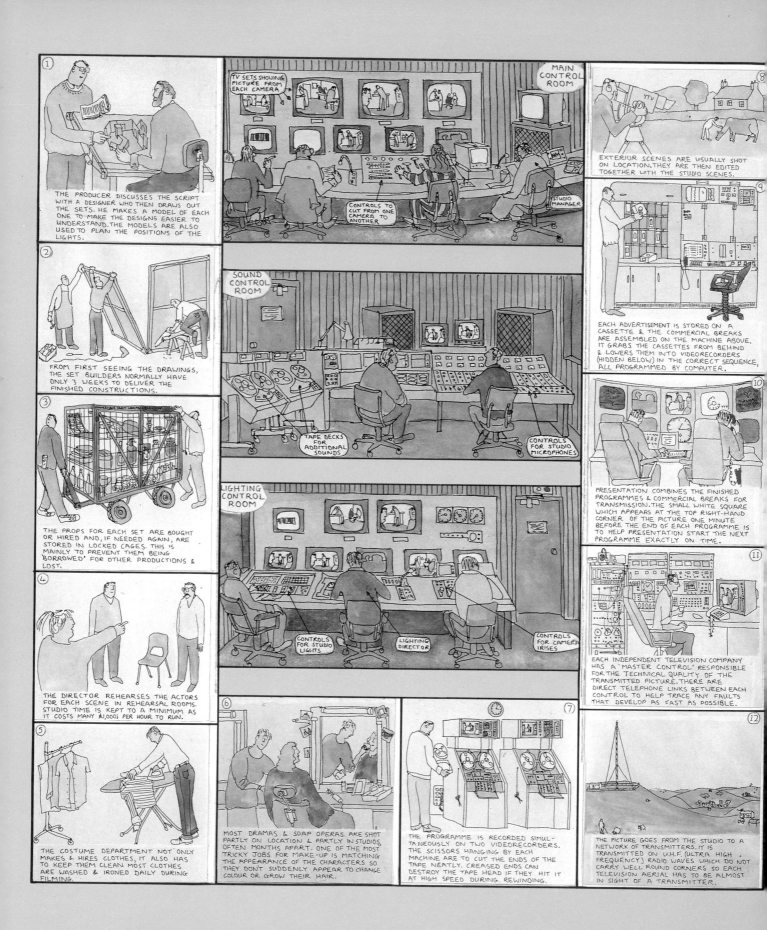

that highlights the complexity of producing a TV drama, particularly one which is shown two nights each week throughout the year.

The advance planning is both vital and time-consuming, for nothing must be overlooked and every eventuality must be foreseen. Once recording begins, everything needed for the many successful 'takes' must be on hand and available; everyone and everything must be in exactly the right place at precisely the right time. Delays through bad organisation and sloppy planning are both expensive and time-consuming; they are also annoying to the cast and crew and so they are not allowed to happen!

Before the scenes are recorded in Studio 3, a camera script is prepared and this lists the sets which are to be featured in a particular recording session. For example, one recording session could include the Woolpack Bar, the back room of the Woolpack Inn, Mrs Bates's cottage lounge, Mrs Bates's cottage kitchen and Home Farm Office. The required sets are therefore built from the scenery which is already in stock and this is done under the supervision of the designer. Hanging around the huge walls are large backcloths painted with outdoor scenes which are hung behind the window openings in the sets. There is the view of some farm buildings from Annie's kitchen door, a view of the main street of Beckindale showing the Woolpack Inn and the view from the windows of the Home Farm Estate Office. The views depicted on these backcloths match the real scenery in the locations where the programme is recorded on Outside Broadcast.

All the items needed for the sequences must be obtained well in advance and in readiness for the recording sessions – even the food is real and when Annie cooks a breakfast, she prepares a proper one on the studio cooker from a menu suggested by the cast! They love Annie's breakfasts! Having built, say, these five sets, all the scenes which are to take place within them will then be recorded according to a pre-arranged timetable. Therefore, these scenes do not follow in the same sequence as the viewers see them when they finally appear on the screen.

For this reason, anyone outside the production team who might be observing a recording session would not be able to follow in sequence the stages of the story. The story is recorded in blocks of six episodes, each episode (with advertisements before, during and after the screening) being of around half an hour's duration when on screen. One director will be employed to direct each block of six scripts. Half the story is recorded on location and half is within Studio 3; this means that all the scenes which take place in the bar of the Woolpack Inn during those six episodes will be recorded one after the other, thus making full use of the set when it has been built. This also applies to the other sets – all those which take place in Annie Sugden's kitchen or Demdyke Cottage or Home Farm Estate Office will be recorded one after the other.

When that particular recording session is over, the set will be demolished and another will take its place on the floor of Studio 3. As a consequence, the floor space used by Annie's kitchen one week might well be the back room of the Woolpack the following week ... albeit with a change of walls, furniture, ornaments and other artefacts. But when it all appears on screen, who would know?

As we view the latest episode in Annie Sugden's life, we join her in the kitchen at Emmerdale Farm in Beckindale – not on the floor of a crowded studio somewhere in Leeds. . . .

A typical studio recording session begins at 9.30am; the artistes are called to the studio where they are made-up to appear before the cameras when required. In the control room with its bank of nine monitors, four of which are linked to the four cameras operating simultaneously from different angles on the floor, the production assistant is at a console with its array of lights and switches, and the vision mixer prepares to identify the images which we will see on our screens out of the many recorded here today. . . .

On the floor of the studio are about thirty members of the production crew including the director upon whose shoulders rests the task of drawing the very best of performances from the artistes and the production team. The floor manager guides the progress of the recording while the four cameras move around like huge silent monsters, seeking their position for a very special shot. Sound technicians sit upon wheeled tripods, the extended noses of their booms jutting into the set with a microphone dangling at the far end, a vital piece of apparatus which must remain close to the actors but which must never appear in shot.

The designer is on hand to supervise the appearance of the sets and the position of the furniture and props while make-up specialists, costumers, the technical supervisor, lighting director, those involved in acquiring and arranging the props or the scenes, the stage manager and assistant stage manager all await their particular task as the recording begins. There are one or two rehearsals before attempting a 'take', the artistes have been called in and are in position on the set, the cameras and control room staff are standing by, the lighting has been adjusted, microphones are checked for sound level . . . there is a tenseness now in the studio because everything that follows must be exactly right. If it means recording many 'takes' before a scene is judged perfect by the director, then those takes will be recorded again and again with patience and good humour. The final one, when it appears on screen, must have no defect of any kind.

The viewer probably sees a few seconds on the screen and thinks it has taken a correspondingly few seconds to record it, but it takes a full week of very hard and dedicated work by as many as sixty people to produce the two half-hour episodes that appear on screen, not forgetting the three secretaries in the 'Emmerdale Farm' office, the team of writers, the script editor and the story editor.

But in Studio 3, recording is about to start. In the control room, three screens marked Cam 1, Cam 2 and Cam 3 show that three of the possible four cameras are operating and on the monitor is the picture the viewers will eventually see. There is a lot of technical chat and preparation between the control room and the floor – this could almost be the control room at an airport or in a fire station or police headquarters.

At this point, the scene being recorded is in Mrs Bates's kitchen where her son, Nick, and his pal, Archie the Beckindale revolutionary left-winger, are clearly involved in some shady escapade involving hens' eggs. Archie is currently living at Mrs Bates's cottage now that Kathy has married Jackie Merrick, and we see Nick and Archie surrounded by dozens of hens' eggs.

Among the cameras, lighting and sound equipment in Studio 3 are recognisable features of Annie's kitchen at Emmerdale Farm. Here, Jack decides the place settings at table.

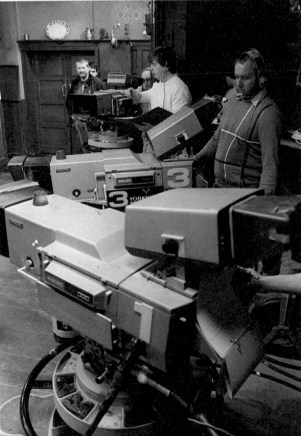

Camermen prepare to record a scene in the Woolpack Inn.

They are washing them and checking for bad ones by using a candle flame to highlight dud yolks. During the rehearsals we learn that they are taking eggs from the nests of hens which are laying away from their nest boxes – Archie feels he has a right to these eggs even though the hens are owned by Emmerdale Farm, although he is prepared to buy some cheap if necessary.

But their enterprise takes an unexpected and delightful turn when some of the eggs hatch. For this sequence the production team had to acquire eggs which were on the point of hatching so that the cameras could record the new chicks emerging from their shells. And the chicks performed right on cue....

A spare supply was on hand, just in case these scenes required several takes and several hatching chickens. Inevitably, Mrs Bates senses that the lads are up to no good; she realises this when they are very quiet one morning as they are eating boiled eggs, but it is some time later when a chick emerges from inside Archie's sweater that she begins to understand their doubtful scheme for selling eggs.

This scene required several takes and the two young actors consumed many eggs before it was acceptable to the producer. As said by Tony Pitts, the actor who plays Archie, 'It's a good job we're not doing a scene involving rhubarb....'

Upon completion of all the scenes in Mrs Bates's kitchen, it is now the turn of Home Farm Estate Office during which several scenes will be shot. In these there are hilarious exchanges between those two protagonists Alan Turner and Seth Armstrong. Turner is now a partner with Joe Sugden in the Home Farm

The clothes worn by the cast are provided from the comprehensive wardrobe of Yorkshire Television. Here is a selection from the mobile wardrobe vehicle which attends all outside broadcasts of 'Emmerdale Farm'.

Estate enterprise, and Seth is continuing in his role as a gamekeeper, roguish and cunning, and always on the scrounge....

In these scenes three walls of Home Farm Estate Office will be in the shot, and so a third wall is swiftly brought on to the set and placed in position. Mrs Bates's desk is placed before it and then she and Alan Turner rehearse their lines.

In this sequence Alan Turner has lost his voice due to a cold and he is dosing himself with pills and potions because he is to address the Skipdale Chamber of Commerce.

His job is to explain to the Chamber the facilities offered by Home Farm Estate. Furthermore, he has lost his driving licence because he was caught driving after drinking too much alcohol, and then Seth enters. Seth wants time off to visit the dentist for a fitting of some new false teeth and he wants them to look as good as Turner's ... Turner is horrified, for he has no false teeth!

Inevitably, Turner loses his voice just before going to make his speech, and there follows a hilarious sequence of events with the voiceless Turner trying to make both Seth and Mrs Bates understand him. By this stage of the day's recording, everyone on the set (actors and production crew) is mimicking the voiceless Turner's hoarse attempts to speak when they are not actually recording ... the result is one of the most fun-filled afternoons and everyone is in fits of laughter at the wonderful acting and the exchanges, both on camera and off, between Seth and Turner. As one cameraman chuckled, 'This is better than the situation comedy they're recording next door!' To see the two men acting out their battling roles, it is difficult to imagine that off screen they are

Time for lunch. In the farmyard of Emmerdale, cast and production crew enjoy a break for a welcome meal.

67

the best of friends, and sometimes during their socialising, Richard Thorp will become Alan Turner and snap at Stan Richards, 'Get out, Seth!'

During this wonderful example of the 'Emmerdale' friendliness, Seth came into the office before his cue, at which Richard Thorp, in his Turner voice, said, 'You haven't come in yet, Seth!'

'I have,' grinned Stan in Seth's voice.

'Get out, Seth!' said Turner. . . .

But then, in spite of all the hilarity, it is time to record this delightful scene. The floor manager calls for total silence and begins his countdown. Ten, nine, eight . . . and then 'Action' and the sheer professionalism of the entire team rises to the fore and a superb 'take' of this memorable scene is completed. It later transpired that many Yorkshire TV personnel in other parts of the huge building had seen this on their own monitors and had thoroughly enjoyed the performance. As a member of the production crew said, 'There is a buoyancy on the floor today – and that's saying something for five o'clock on a Friday afternoon!'

And suddenly it was all over. The day's recording had been completed on schedule and it was time for the artistes and crew to go home. The studio lights went out, the cameras and recording equipment were switched off and everyone began to leave Studio 3. And then the scene shifters moved in. . . .

Within a very short time every scrap of evidence of 'Emmerdale Farm' had been removed. The studio was a big empty space; it was time to prepare it for the recording of another programme.

On Location

There is a saying in North Yorkshire that March is a month of many weathers. In other words, anything can be expected – we can experience everything from sunshine to blizzards – and it was during 1988 upon an unsettled day in this most unpredictable of months that the production team arrived at Emmerdale Farm to record a selection of outdoor scenes.

It is a boast that the weather, however awkward and severe, has never halted the outdoor work, nor has it ever stopped an OB, as an Outside Broadcast on location is known. After all, life in the open air, both around the farm and in the glorious Yorkshire Dales, is such a vital ingredient in the 'Emmerdale' story that the notoriously unpredictable British climate must not dictate the course of events. To steal a phrase from theatre lore, the show must go on.

Snow has been hosed from the roofs and roads to give the appearance of spring; there have been occasions when frozen snow has been covered with compost or sand to give the appearance of bare earth and there have been times the actors have faced conditions so cold that their faces have frozen as they tried to say their lines. Freak snow storms in the late spring have caused havoc with recording sessions, producing snow in one scene and fresh green fields in the subsequent one. On the other hand, when a rain storm was required for one scene, the sun just refused to stop shining – and so hoses had to be brought in to supply the necessary downpour.

It is not surprising, therefore, that the entire cast and production team of 'Emmerdale Farm' have the reputation for being as tough and determined as the Yorkshire character they portray so well.

'I thought this pen was for our lambs to be kept in ...'

On this March day, which was to test them thoroughly, the morning's work had started very early with the first of the Outside Broadcast vehicles leaving the Yorkshire TV studios in Leeds at 7.30am. A twelve-seater mini-bus had been hired to convey the staff of the make-up and costume departments to Emmerdale Farm, a half-hour journey into the countryside of North Yorkshire. Other vehicles included the fleet of OB transporters, one of them being the generator vehicle which is affectionately known as Genny. Genny is needed when recording sequences are some distance from a source of electricity – and in some remote parts of the Dales there is no electricity within miles.

When travelling to an OB location, everything that is needed for the day's recording must be transported from the studios. There are the cameras, lights, sound equipment, miles of cable, the vehicle containing the costumes, the make-up and the canteen vehicle with its refreshment facilities and enough food and drink for the day.

Also on site by 7.30am were four artistes' caravans with heating and lighting. These provided the artistes with private accommodation for costume changes as well as very welcome rest facilities.

One large van contained the portable props which were required and another

What does the future hold for Joe and Ruth (Julia Chambers)? Here is a moment of contemplation between them as they discuss their plans.

brought a mass of technical equipment used for monitoring and recording the day's events. Added to this was an assortment of cars or vans that were to be used during the scenes; two horses (one for Alan Turner to ride and one for Joe Sugden), a caravan for use by two Yuppies who were visiting the Dales, Archie's tumbledown caravan, a concrete mixer, a tractor bearing a fearsome front attachment ... and all these were parked among the familiar buildings of Emmerdale Farm.

Having secured all the support vehicles, a fleet of hire cars and taxis had been booked to convey the artistes to the farm, although some used their own transport. Making sure everyone and everything is on location is a massive and important undertaking; it has to include everything from the cars or other vehicles used in the story to minor objects like the eggs that Annie might carry, the cereals Archie might have for his breakfast in his lonely caravan or the famous woolly hat worn by Seth Armstrong. Nothing is left to chance; every detail, however small, is meticulously planned in advance.

Ensuring that every required piece of equipment arrives at the right place at the right time involves highly efficient administration and organisation. In the 'Emmerdale' suite at the Yorkshire TV offices, capable secretaries work busily to make sure nothing is overlooked. Everyone involved with the day's shooting is issued with a call sheet which details the requirements and lists the shooting order of the scenes. It names the artistes who will take part and the times they must be on the set as well as the additional requirements such as vehicles, animals and other necessities. It also forms an *aide-mémoire* because it will contain reminders about the additional effects needed for each scene, even down to things like the tyre marks that will be left by the vehicles in the fields if they are to feature in the storyline.

The designer plans each scene with detailed drawings which show the positions of artistes, vehicles, animals, stationary objects and technical equipment.

By 8.30am, the production team had arrived at Emmerdale Farm. This comprised around thirty-five people and on this day it included a trained nurse and a safety officer because a dangerous scene involving the destruction of Archie's caravan was due to be shot.

As this assembly of people and vehicles was preparing for its day at Emmerdale Farm, the work of the real farm continued. In the fields tiny lambs, some but a few days old, were huddling close to their mothers against the chill winds.

A domestic goose with just a hint of the wild greylag in her plumage was sitting on her nest near the stream which runs through the farm, hens were scratching around the yard and a curlew was calling somewhere among the clouds which carried the threat of March's unpredictable mood. And Farmer Arthur Bell was working in his outbuildings, apparently oblivious to the enormous activity that surrounded him and his farm.

At the start of this working day the weather brightened and bathed the landscape in fleeting patches of brilliant sunshine; it patterned this splendid Yorkshire Dale with pools of light which were quickly shaded by the moving clouds, but the wind was not so friendly. Anxiously the production team

The cramped interior of the mobile control room. This vehicle accompanies the outside broadcast crews when they are recording on location.

looked to the skies and examined the distant view to the west for signs of oncoming storms.

There had been a backlog of scenes from the previous day and this had to be cleared before the scheduled programme could be completed. Dennis Elliott, the unit manager, an imposing figure with his thick white hair and beard, was seated in the Emmerdale hay barn among a conglomeration of lights, cameras and sound equipment. Even so, all this was almost hidden among the paraphernalia of a working farm – oil cans, hay, disused machinery, ploughs, etc.

In this scene, Jack Sugden helped Matt and Dolly cover a pine Welsh dresser Dolly had bought for the new home she had so desperately wanted at Crossgill, an unexpected but welcome legacy from a hermit-like character befriended by Matt.

In the midst of Dolly's sorrow, Jackie arrived in a battered Citroen, bubbling with enthusiasm over plans to purchase a house which would be a new home for him and his young wife, Kathy.

The scenes which are recorded during one day at the farm location do not follow the same progression of the story; several are shot in the farm buildings because of the length of time it takes to set up all the equipment – lighting, cameras and sound, for example – and these are later edited into their correct sequence. Polaroid photographs are taken at the end of each recorded scene for continuity purposes. Because subsequent scenes may be recorded much later in, say, the studio, it is vital that the appearance of the artistes at the end of one scene matches their appearance at the beginning of the next. For example, if Annie has windswept hair and snow on her shoulders as she opens the door which leads into her kitchen from the farm yard, then she must look exactly the same during the following scene when she is actually seen inside her kitchen and closing the door in the heat of the Leeds studio a week later.

And so, because it was milking time on this real farm, the next scene was in the mistle, the Yorkshire name for the cow house. The Emmerdale herd of British Friesians was ushered into the building, each slow-moving cow finding her own stall with its covering of clean straw, a trough of hay and a little water fountain which the cow could activate with her nose.

Farmer Bell tethered each animal as the production team moved in to film a scene involving two young city people caravanning near by. The mistle looks like any other Dales cow shed, but in the rafters, a range of permanent scaffolding is strategically placed to support a battery of TV lighting equipment. In seconds, the mistle was full of cameras, lights, cables, microphones, people doing important jobs, and that mass of essential subsidiary equipment. The cows did not mind at all; in the calm atmosphere of the mistle, they chewed their cud as the team prepared to shoot their scenes.

This was a fine example of the remarkable co-operation that exists between Farmer Bell of the real farm, and the mass of people who help create the fictitious Emmerdale Farm. The work of the real farm must not be interrupted and so the televising of the 'Emmerdale' story is accommodated within Mr Bell's own busy timetable. The shooting began with a short rehearsal by Jack and Matt, and two city yuppies who acted so convincingly that all thought they were genuinely baffled by country life. They even refused a drink of fresh milk obtained direct from one of Emmerdale's placid bovine stars.

During the shooting, one of the cows tried to upstage the actors by rattling the chain that was loosely fastened around her neck . . . a crew member had to hold her head until the scene had been shot, and she made no further protest. Once the scene was completed, the cows were milked and their equipment dismantled as everyone broke off for coffee.

In Yorkshire, this mid-morning break is called 'lowance time and after ten minutes, it was time to venture into the fields for scenes involving Archie's famous caravan with its rainbow colour scheme and its accompanying heap of domestic rubbish. After savouring the warmth and shelter of the mistle, all the equipment, technicians and artistes involved then had to endure the uncertain March weather in a lofty field without shelter on the slopes of a Yorkshire dale.

Much of the expensive and heavy equipment was lugged up the slope by hand and it was now that the true ferocity of the weather made itself felt. During the filming in the hay barn and the mistle, the driving rain had been avoided, and those early morning patches of sunlight had been swept into oblivion by the strengthening winds. As the production team attempted to establish themselves for the scene, the sky blackened high in the dale and within minutes a driving blizzard of sleet and hail swept across the landscape. Everyone huddled under their anoraks, umbrellas and waterproofs as the driving rain saturated any exposed areas.

Several attempts were made to shoot this scene; actress Jean Rogers (Dolly) tried so hard to conclude her speeches; Tony Pitts (Archie Brooks) tried time and time again to write his slogan YIPIS – Yorkshire Independence Party and International Socialists – on the side of his caravan.

Archie's colourful caravan, seconds after it had been struck by a tractor driven by his pal Nick Bates.

Meanwhile, Cy Chadwick (Nick Bates) waited to drive the tractor into the side of Archie's caravan and wreck it ... a dramatic moment in the story.

But this time the March weather was conspiring against 'Emmerdale Farm'. Time and time again the production team attempted to shoot these scenes and time and time again a fresh storm, so ferocious but so blessedly short, swept across the fields to prevent them. Hail, sleet, snow and rain lashed the crew and all their equipment as sheep and their tiny lambs huddled for shelter behind the dry-stone walls.

The curlews stopped their warbling and the sodden crew simply waited, showing remarkable patience and determination to complete their work. As unit manager Dennis Elliott said, 'We don't aim to please; we aim to finish.' And how they tried. But, as director Terry Daw was to discover, the strength of the wind made the cameras unstable; even the combined weight of two large men could not render them steady enough to record the scenes; the driving rain was finding its way into the equipment, the artistes were getting soaked and a check with the Met. Office showed that there was to be no break in the weather for the rest of that day.

Reluctantly, and for the first time in the experience of many team members, the day's shooting had to be abandoned. Dennis Elliott gave the instruction to 'Wrap', the word for the termination of the day's recording.

This was in direct contrast to another day's recording out of doors. Although the weather was dry and bright, the day was to present its own nail-biting drama as it fully tested the extraordinary skills of the special effects team.

74

On a brilliantly sunny day in April, albeit with a biting wind direct from the fells, the production team was to record the dramatic and heart-breaking fire which destroyed the old farm house at Crossgill and, with it, Dolly Skilbeck's dreams.

The location of Crossgill is superb; the old farm stands on the side of a remote part of Beckindale's westerly fells with extensive views along the dale. The Outside Broadcast vehicles had arrived at 7.30am to find peace around Crossgill, with skylarks dancing musically above and a pair of kestrels hovering near by. The full complement of Outside Broadcast vehicles had arrived, including Genny, the generator vehicle, the mobile canteen, artistes' caravans, mobile loos, props vehicle, which had to carry everything from a cement mixer to a penknife, the make-up caravan, the scanner, the mobile control room, technicians' vehicles full of sound equipment, lighting equipment, cameras, miles of cable and all that goes with highly complex requirements of an Outside Broadcast for a drama serial; there were buses to ferry the crews, cars which had brought countless other workers ranging from the nurse and safety officer who may be needed if things went wrong, a realistic-looking police car and bicycles for use by the extras who would form a small knot of bystanders as the fire raged.

For this recording, the personnel numbered about seventy, and later in the day as the fire sequences were recorded, the North Yorkshire Fire Brigade from Harrogate would be required, as would many of the characters who were central to the unfolding drama. Some were also needed for recording sequences in the studio at Leeds, and as this day's shooting began, the crew was half a day behind due to unforeseen difficulties earlier in the week.

The key to the whole operation was the fire. Yorkshire TV's special effects expert, Kevin Christie, had spent days working out his requirements for these scenes, and had spent a further three days at the derelict house, setting up the equipment required to produce the realistic blaze. Behind the farm house, out of range of the cameras, was a tiered platform of scaffolding upon which were about twenty gas canisters with long tubes attached, bales of straw, pieces of wood, old tyres and masses of other combustible material. Additional props were frames of silver foil – these were about six feet high and eight feet long, rather like portable frames used for hanging clothes. Dangling from the top rail were strips of heavy tin foil which rustled in the strong breezes of the dale; these were placed inside the house and when the fire effect was needed, a powerful red light would shine from behind each of these rails. It would reflect upon the walls and within the rooms, and the movement of the foil would give the appearance of flickering flames.

But there was to be real fire, too, controlled by experts but real, none-the-less, and another additional effect was the smoke. This was to be produced from smoke pots; the smoke is really fine dust which is forced from the pots to make a very realistic cloud of smoke. There were fifty-six smoke pots, each of which lasted two minutes, and several would be used simultaneously at different points within the house. These were the only smoke pots available, so the fire scenes had to be recorded before these were exhausted. There was ample for an ordinary day's recording – but recording stage-managed fires on the slopes of the Yorkshire Pennines on a gusty April day is hardly 'ordinary'!

The smoke which was to appear outside the house would come from the burning straw and tyres.

One continuing problem was that the fire had to be switched on and off at frequent intervals because it was needed for a range of other scenes; it must be controlled too, because it must not be allowed to burn down the house and it must be available when required for the many scenes in which it had to feature. A further hazard was that some scenes at Crossgill did not require a fire and so evidence of the blaze had to be concealed until it was needed.

One additional hazard was the blustery April wind; on the slopes of this beautiful dale, it was fluctuating wildly in both strength and direction, the very thing that was NOT wanted during the recording of these difficult scenes.

Earlier, there had been scenes to establish the story – Annie arriving at the deserted farm and admiring the view, the flickering blaze inside where Phil Pearce had been working, Annie reaching the top of the stairs, the whoosh of flames when the draught caught the fire, the exploding gas cylinder which blew out the windows and Annie struggling downstairs to find the front door jammed. She is trapped in the blazing house.

Other scenes recorded that morning included Sandie and Dolly driving out to the farm and finding it ablaze as they arrive at the farm gate. Annie's car is parked near by. They realise she is inside the burning house ... Phil Pearce returns in his old van ... he smashes down the door and rescues Annie.... During several short scenes of this kind, fire and smoke is required to create the right effect, including some long-distance shots of the blazing building. There are several 'takes' of these scenes, all consuming precious smoke cans and fire-producing gas. But all these scenes, which are recorded out of the sequence in which they will appear on screen, have to be completed before the dramatic fire itself is recorded. And each was recorded in those blustery conditions.

During the shooting, a real-life drama was being enacted near by. The farmer who had allowed this empty house to be used as Crossgill had a cow which had become sick and was lying in a stone building only yards from the fire. As the recording was in progress, the veterinary surgeon arrived to visit his patient.

He had to be allowed access through the conglomeration of vehicles and people. A North Yorkshire policeman was on duty and patrolled the lane near the farm; his task was to ensure that traffic would flow and that genuine bystanders did not hamper those who wished to pass along the lane, and that they did not intrude upon the recording. The vet arrived and the recording was halted as he was guided through this uncharacteristic countryside crowd of people and vehicles; he managed to reach the sick cow to carry out his treatment – this was a real countryside story, but it could have been a scene from 'Emmerdale Farm'.

All the shorter scenes in which the fire featured were recorded before lunch, all consuming precious smoke and gas; after lunch came the major portion of this part of the 'Emmerdale' story. A crowd of about twenty extras had been assembled to act as bystanders, but the earlier smoke and activity had attracted a genuine crowd of bystanders, who had to be kept at a distance for technical reasons.

Main picture: *Crossgill on fire. The crowd comprised cast and extras who played the part of family, friends and bystanders who watched helplessly as the house blazed.*

Inset: *As the fire raged in the bedroom of Crossgill, a gas canister exploded to spread the fire and blow out the window. And Annie Sugden was trapped inside.*

The Fire Brigade had arrived too. This was a real fire appliance from Harrogate, kept as a reserve vehicle and used for training purposes; it had been hired for the recording and the firemen were all reserves who had volunteered for this task. Also in the scene were a policeman and a police-woman who arrived in the fake police car, while the real constable continued his duty near by.

The director, unit manager, designer, stage manager and chief cameraman then had the difficult task of positioning all the artistes, extras and equipment in their precise positions for the recording of this important scene; three cameras were to be used simultaneously and the fire had to appear exactly on cue when it was required, with lots of accompanying flame and smoke. The Fire Brigade had to rush to the scene with ladders and hoses to extinguish the blaze; their participation was for the benefit of the story only, for Kevin Christie was quite capable of extinguishing his own blaze. And so the gleaming red fire appliance was parked in position, ready for action.

All the participants in this scene were ready for the first rehearsal which would be followed by several 'takes' until the scene was recorded in precisely the right way for eventual transmission on the screen. The woodwork of the windows and doors of Crossgill had been coated with a fire-resistant gel, although it was felt that the heat generated by the fake fire would burst the glass in the windows.

But there were problems. The shifting wind had blown the 'smoke' to the back of the house and out of camera range, and this had resulted in an unexpectedly high consumption of smoke pots and fire-producing gas as efforts were made to record suitable pictures.

The difficulties of this day's recording had almost exhausted the stock of smoke cans, and, for the same reason, the carefully calculated gas supply had almost run out. It was known that the only suitable smoke cans available in the whole of England were in Kent – where there were four. The Fire Brigade did have their own supplies, but these were too noisy for this particular use. It would take days to get the right materials. The only solution was to perform this scene in just one take, with no rehearsal. If this failed, there would be no smoke for any subsequent recordings of the scene – and just enough gas for one more take of the blazing house.

This meant that every smallest action by the artistes, the extras, the camera crew, sound engineers, lighting experts, those in charge of the fire inside the house, and the real fire officers, had to be exactly right first time. Everything must happen at precisely the right moment.

There could be no second chance, no re-takes, no excuses.

As the magnitude of this demand dawned upon the assembly in the paddock of Crossgill, the ultimate responsibility rested upon the director, Terry Daw. He checked everything and everyone, double-checking the equipment, the fire-creating apparatus, the strength and direction of the unpredictable wind, the position of the artistes and extras, the sound levels, the cameras, the background of the countryside to ensure nothing unwanted had crept in, and the timing of everyone's own particular part in this highly charged moment.

Smoke is generated at the rear of the house.

Everyone and everything was still; there was not a movement in that valley

as Terry Daw made his final preparations. When he shouted 'Action' there would be no halting the recording and no second chance to get it right.

In an atmosphere of high tension, he shouted 'Action', and for yet another occasion that day the onlookers saw Crossgill ablaze. Flames poured from the windows upstairs and downstairs, they crept along the gutters and they burst into searing tongues of fire and smoke around the doorway.

From behind the house, masses of billowing black smoke rose into the clear blue sky while inside, everything was aglow. The cameras recorded this scene as the Sugdens and the Skilbecks, with their neighbours and friends around them, stood in awe and shock as Dolly's dream vanished in that mass of smoke and flames. Everyone acting in this episode had to show their deep understanding of just how close to death Annie had been, and how a major disaster had almost been created by that fire. On cue, the firemen brought their hoses and put on a very realistic fire-fighting display until the flames of Crossgill were conquered. Kevin Christie, who was inside the house during every one of the day's recordings, switched off his gas, but his smoke supply was exhausted.

The fire was out and when Terry Daw shouted 'Cut' everyone applauded. This was the very best example of recording on location; this most difficult and important of scenes had been achieved in just one take.

And then, as if by magic, the wind dropped and hot sunshine bathed the landscape as the birds began to sing.

It was a day of drama on the Yorkshire fells, one which will be retold many times in the studios of Yorkshire Television and in the crowded bar of the famous Woolpack Inn, Beckindale.

Matt comforts Dolly after the loss of Crossgill.

79

Even the youngest cows can be obtinate at times!

When Jenny the donkey brayed, it upset the recording sessions in Beckindale, and so she was written into the story. Seth won her in a game of dominoes!

Young Sam loves to work with the animals, especially the lambs.

One of Dolly's jobs on the farm involves looking after the poultry. Here she is with some delightful day-old chicks.

Jack and Pat with Pat's goat, which escaped from the farm.

Matt's sheepdog, Nell, is invaluable in his work as a sheperd on the fells.

Chapter Four

Gazetteer

Beckindale

Beckindale is one of North Yorkshire's smaller dales and, in common with many of its size, does not feature on most tourist or motorists' maps. This pretty dale has given its name to the village (pop. 575) which stands mid-way between the Dalehead and the Dale End. This is a feature of several Yorkshire dales, such as Rosedale and Colsterdale.

Situated in the foothills of the Pennines, the valley of Beckindale has always been noted for its fertility; this stems from the Neolithic period when the dale, and many others in this region, were a network of lakes. The present landscape was probably formed some two million years ago, since when there has been a succession of Ice Ages alternating with periods of great warmth. The melting glaciers sculpted the distinctive dales and hills and the vanished lakes have left a legacy of fertile green valleys, or Dales as they are known in northern England.

Deep below the surface of the Dales is a complex of underground limestone caves whose entrances formed the home of Stone Age dwellers when they first came to these Dales. It is known that New Stone Age people occupied the land we now call Beckindale within the last ten thousand years. By the Neolithic period they had learned to make simple tools and to cultivate the land; they could spin wool, weave cloth and make pottery and had learned to breed cattle and grow cereals.

Relics of early man's presence can still be seen on the moors which surround Beckindale, chiefly in the form of burial mounds or tumuli, sometimes called howes. Because of the marshy nature of the lowlands, they occupied the high ground but as the waters of those early lakes gradually receded, the people moved deeper into the valley where they began to cultivate the rich legacy of highly fertile soil.

Few records remain of Beckindale's early history. It is known, however, that the Brigantes led by King Venutius settled on the slopes of Ingleborough some distance to the north-west of Beckindale. They were wealthy due to early lead mining in the Dales and they led a highly sophisticated life. But they were defeated in battles with the invading Romans and lost their power in, and

claim to, these Dales. There is some evidence of a Roman settlement in Beckindale; fragments of pottery, glass and red Samian ware were found in 1922 during renovations to the Old Hall which is now a farm house.

Beckindale's more recent history can be traced to Danish and Viking settlers as the name implies. 'Beck' is a northern term for a stream or brook, having links with the Danish 'baek' or the Old Norse 'bekkr'. 'Dale' is a northern word for a valley and similar words are widely used in Scandinavia. The word 'dale' has mixed origins, coming variously from words like 'dael' in both Old Saxon and Old Norse. It features extensively in the names of Yorkshire villages, near-by Skipdale being just one example but it is essentially Scandinavian in its origin.

Early records of Beckindale show that the stream which flows through the village was once known simply as The Beck in the Dale, later being corrupted into T'beck in t'Dale and eventually Beckindale. This gave its name to the valley and to the village which is now the focus of the Dales community. Today, however, the stream is called Nun's Beck; research has identified the site of a former Benedictine nunnery in a field beside the beck, below Demdyke Row and the cricket field. The nuns used it for their water supply and walked beside it in silent contemplation. The nunnery was destroyed during the Reformation and no evidence remains, although a field beside the beck is still known as Nun's Meadow.

Beckindale today.

Overleaf: *An artist's impression of Beckindale.*

83

To Hotten

To Littlewell

Gimbels' Farm

Police Station

Woolpack Inn

Emmerdale Farm

BECKINDALE
A Village and its People

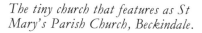

The tiny church that features as St Mary's Parish Church, Beckindale.

Every autumn the Parish Church is filled with the fruits of the harvest as the villagers give thanks for yet another successful year. After the service, the fruit and vegetables which have been used to decorate the church are given to local charities. Here, some of the produce is on display before the altar.

The church of St Mary occupies one of the oldest sites in Beckindale; this has been a centre of worship for centuries as testified by ancient yews in the churchyard. It is known that the Saxons had a wooden church on the site, but the Normans rebuilt it in stone and traces of their work can still be seen in the arch leading into the nave and traces of a Norman doorway in the north wall. The font is also Norman. The church underwent massive structural modifications in the sixteenth century, while the rood screen is thought to be seventeenth century. Some of the exterior tracery work is a delight although further renovations in the nineteenth century have obliterated much of the church's earlier history. An ancient glass window shows the figure of St Paul, and the pulpit was carved by Italian craftsmen during the sixteenth century.

A view of the main street in Beckindale. The Woolpack Inn is on the right in the distance.

Al Dixon who played the part of the silent Walter, a regular in the Woolpack Inn.

The church contains the tombs of the early de Verniers later known as the Verneys, squires of Beckindale from 1588 until 1979.

Other buildings of historic interest include the Vicarage, *c*.1823 and the village hall, *c*.1923. The present school was built in 1807 and bears the inscription 'THIS SCHOOL WAS ERECTED BY VOLUNTARY SUBSCRIPTION AD MDCCCVII. TRAIN UP A CHILD IN THE WAY HE SHOULD GO AND WHEN HE IS OLD HE WILL NOT DEPART FROM IT'. The old police station was constructed in 1856 and formally opened by the Mayor of Hotten, Alderman M. A. Boothroyd. This is now a private house, Beckindale being policed from Hotten.

There are two inns in Beckindale, the Malt Shovel Inn and the Woolpack; it is said that author Charles Kingsley stayed overnight in the building now known as the Woolpack Inn during his journey to Malham Cove and Tarn, a visit which inspired his famous book, *The Water Babies*, published in 1863. The earlier Woolpack Inn, built *c.*1776, is now a private dwelling house.

The sports complex, which includes a tennis court, bowling green, cricket field and club house, was a gift to the village by the Verney Estate, and since the closure of that estate it has been managed by trustees on behalf of the community. The village hall was also built for the village by the Verney Estate, the cost being shared equally by the Estate and the village people who raised funds by subscription and events of many kinds.

The cottages of Beckindale are, without exception, constructed in the traditional grey stone of the region with blue/grey tiled roofs. Many were constructed by the Estate for its employees and when NY Estates purchased the Verney Estate, it also acquired most of the property in the village. Several homes were purchased by the occupiers, and today some of the Beckindale cottages remain in the hands of Joe Sugden and Alan Turner, the new owners of the Estate, now called Home Farm.

No new property has been constructed in Beckindale for many years, any proposed development being carefully monitored by the Yorkshire Dales National Park and the local council. There are no brick houses or bungalows, for example.

The largest farm in the village is Emmerdale Farm, a mixed holding of some 300 acres; its name comes from emmer, a species of wheat which has always flourished in this dale.

Connelton

Connelton lies west of Beckindale and is a larger village (pop. 1,367) whose origins date to the Danes and Vikings. The suffix 'ton' comes from the Scandinavian 'tun' meaning a farm, and the prefix 'Connel' may derive from the old Danish family name of Kundi or from the old West Scandinavian name Kunda. Some early references show the name as 'Kundatun', 'Kunaltun', 'Cundeltun' and 'Cundleton'.

Another possibility is that the prefix comes from the Old English 'cuna' meaning cows and that 'cuna-tun' meant cow farm.

An old guide described the village as having 'many natural charms', for it is a sprawling village built on the sides of steep fells. The rows of stone terrace cottages with blue slate roofs date to the early lead miners who populated this district.

Lead mining began around Connelton with the Brigantes and then the Romans, much of the hewing being done by convicts from a near-by Roman penal colony. It continued in a small way through the succeeding centuries, some lead from these mines being used to line the roof of St Peter's in Rome, and much being utilised for the roofing of many Yorkshire abbeys. Some fine examples of minerals from these mines can be seen in the Natural History Museum in London.

Modern commercial mining started during the last century when the London

Lead Company secured the rights to these ancient mines, and this brought a massive influx of people to the hamlet of Connelton. Two churches were built, several inns constructed, as well as the Reading Room, village hall, many terrace houses and commercial properties such as banks and trading centres. During this reconstruction, many medieval buildings were demolished, the stone being used for the new structures.

Connelton lead mining reached its peak between 1850 and 1870, after which it declined until it ended during the First World War.

The Old Mill on the banks of Connelton Beck has now been converted into private dwellings, having lain derelict for almost forty years. This was an early cotton mill, constructed around 1783 to cater for the influx of cotton following the American War of Independence; the raw materials were brought to Connelton by pack-horse from the Lancastrian ports. As the woollen industry superseded cotton in this area, the mill was converted into a woollen mill, but suffered from the fierce competition of larger mills in the region. It closed in 1923 and was one of the first mills to be operated by electricity. After closing, it was utilised for a time as a warehouse for animal feeds, later falling into disrepair.

Today the village attracts shoppers and business people from the surrounding Dales who use it as a pleasant commercial and shopping centre. It has one supermarket, a range of shops, restaurants, hostels and garages, with two art galleries, a pottery and two rural craft workshops. Some of the buildings serve as reminders of its short span of commercial mining success, particularly the Lead Master's House near the town centre which is now a small museum (open from Easter until the end of October), while the small park with its miniature lake and collection of water lilies is of particular interest.

Hotten

At the time of the compilation of the Domesday Book, several villages in North Yorkshire were called Hoton or Hotun, the name meaning a tun or farm situated on a hoh or a ridge. In modern terms, this could mean Ridge Farm, but the original tun or farm has usually grown into a village or town. The term 'hoh' meaning ridge now appears in various forms in other names, e.g. Brackenhoe, Howe Bridge, Potto, Binscoe and many others, but the two components 'hoh' and 'tun' have emerged as 'hoton', 'hotun' or more commonly as 'Hutton'.

In many cases the name Hutton has an additional prefix or suffix to identify more clearly the 'farm on the ridge', and examples include Sheriff Hutton, Hutton Conyers, Low Hutton, Hutton Bonville, Hutton-le-Hole, Sand Hutton, Hutton Magna, Hutton Lowcross, Hutton Mulgrave, Hutton Rudby, High Hutton and Huttons Ambo. Throughout England there are some half-dozen Huttons without either a suffix or prefix, and near Loughborough there is a village called Hoton, a clear example of the unchanged use of this name.

Hotten is therefore unique; there is no other known Hotten or Hotton with

Emmerdale Farm is located on one of the beautiful Yorkshire Dales beneath the slopes of the Pennines.

this spelling in the UK and it simply means the farm on the ridge. Hotten with an 'e' is an ancient local spelling which has been adopted by the town after a medieval bishop spelt it in this manner in the parish register of St Crispin's church.

The ridge which has given the town its name overlooks Wharfedale and, as the name suggests, this community stands upon that ridge.

People have dwelt at Hotten for more than a thousand years but few of its ancient ruins are now visible. The woollen industry of the Dales, which itself dates to medieval times, made use of Hotten's central position and accessibility for the establishment of a huge cattle market and wool distribution centre. Hotten Market can trace its history to the twelfth century when sheep breeders in the Dales trekked to Hotten in their hundreds to sell and buy their animals and to trade their wool.

Hotten, then known as Hotun, is recorded in the Domesday Book, and the parish church of St Crispin dates to Norman times. Fragments of some Norman crosses have been constructed within the rebuilt walls of the church and the War Memorial to the men of Hotten who fell in the 1914–18 World War is in the form of such a cross. Much of the church dates from the fourteenth century, with the tower being from the fifteenth and the main structure dating from around 1750. Some of the internal woodwork is Georgian and on some

90

panelling on the west wall is a memorial to Ralph de Vernier, complete with shield and crest. This branch of the de Vernier family were Lords of the Manor of Hotten and Henry Verney was Hotten's first Member of Parliament following the Reform Act of 1832.

The weekly market continues every Friday, as it has since the Middle Ages, where produce, vegetables, fruit and household goods can be purchased from colourful open-air stalls; this market (which is distinct from the cattle market), was established by Royal Charter in 1110 by King Henry I. It attracted the attention of Daniel Defoe when travelling through Yorkshire in the eighteenth century who said it was one of the finest market places of its kind. One of the unusual features is the number of shoemakers and cobblers who continue to attend the market – this custom began in the twelfth century because St Crispin, patron saint of Hotten Parish Church, is also the patron saint of shoemakers.

The annual Bartholomew Fair is held in the market place during the week commencing with St Bartholomew's Day (24 August) when the fairground and its traditional entertainers come to Hotten.

The town is known for the panoramic views from the streets as they overlook Wharfedale, and there is an especially dramatic vista from the Crispin Gardens which adjoin the churchyard. It is claimed that on a very clear day it is possible to see the towers of York Minster and the uprights of the Humber Bridge from there. During the Roman occupation, there was a beacon, signalling station and camp on this site, it then being known as Volusium. Bonfires were lit on these heights to celebrate the British naval victory over the Spanish Armada in 1588 and Nelson's victory at Trafalgar in 1805.

Other points of interest in Hotten include the Wool Exchange, the Corn Exchange (which is now an indoor craft centre), and the new Hotten Everyman Theatre in George Street which regularly stages productions from the finest of modern British playwrights. The art gallery contains a selection of fine portraits in oil, many of which have come from the de Vernier collection, and to the south of the town there is a Weaving Museum in Distaff Row, a pretty street which used to be a row of weavers' cottages.

The market cross is of particular interest; it is not the original, for that was destroyed by a mob in 1534, but a replacement designed by Sir Charles Barry who also designed the Houses of Parliament.

The town's distinctive Dales architecture provides constant inspiration for artists and photographers, while it is widely known for the quality of its many hotels and range of fine restaurants. The town (pop. 12,650) supports a weekly newspaper, the *Hotten Courier*.

Littlewell

A hamlet in the Dales some eight miles to the north-east of Hotten, Littlewell is known for the Littlewell Nature Reserve with its miniature lakes, woodland and marshy areas which support a noted collection of rare orchids and a variety of wild birds. One of the orchids which grows here is the famous Lady's

Above left: *Sheila Mercier and Jean Rogers with the Emmerdale Rose. It was introduced at the 1983 Chelsea Flower Show and can be seen at Nostel Priory Rose Gardens near Wakefield, West Yorkshire.*

Above right: *Amos in his beekeeping days.*

Slipper, thought to be extinct in other parts of Yorkshire, while among the rare birds which have been recorded here are Cetti's Warbler, the Red-backed Shrike and the Golden Oriele.

The name is thought to have derived from Litherwell, meaning the 'land and slope near the well', for the ancient well continues to supply pure spring water. It has never been known to cease flowing.

The hamlet comprises a handful of stone cottages with grey slate roofs in a valley beneath a succession of long grey limestone scars which line the fells behind. There is no parish church, no shop and no public house, although references to Litherwell have been found in some seventeenth-century records. Littlewell is accessible from one direction only, via a gated road leading from the Hotten–Beckindale route, and it lies in a hollow at the head of the dale. It was painted by the great English landscape artist, Turner, when he stayed with Squire Fawkes at near-by Farnley Hall between 1808 and 1825.

Skipdale

One of the most popular of the market towns of the Yorkshire Dales, Skipdale is smaller than the industrial centres of Leeds, Bradford and Halifax, and is slightly smaller than Harrogate. With a population of around 47,000, it is probably best known for the dramatically located Skipdale Castle which over-looks the majestic gorge known as Skipdale Gap. The sides of the gorge are covered by a profuse growth of rhododendrons while the waters of Fell Beck surge through a narrow opening as they descend through the dale to join the river Wharfe to the south of Hotten.

Dating back to the twelfth century and surrounded by a moat, Skipdale Castle was built by the powerful Jorvalle family, with the construction begin-ning around 1135. The original wooden structure is believed to have been replaced by a stone building between 1307 and 1317, but this was destroyed by the Scots in 1322 when the resident Jorvalles fled to safety in Wensleydale and settled in a village now called Jervaulx.

The ruins remained for almost two centuries, until the lands passed into the hands of William de Thornebergh who established a programme of restoration.

He constructed his new castle on the foundations of the old, rebuilding the first and second floors, and adding the east and west turrets, each with a staircase, before embarking on his mammoth task of restoring the Great Chamber. That was finally completed in 1576.

His heir, Charles de Thornebergh, continued his work, remodelling the interior of the castle and adding a fine extension to the west wing, which can still be seen and is open to the public. One of the legends of the castle is that Charles II lived here in great secrecy before his restoration to the throne, when Cromwell and indeed the entire nation thought Charles had fled overseas.

Descendants of the Thornborough family lived here until 1806 when the line died out with the death of Sir Walter Thornborough, who had no heirs. The castle fell into ruin and is now cared for by the English Heritage. The lawns and Great Chamber, with its intricate Jacobean carving, are of particular interest. It is open to the public from 1 April until 30 September each year.

Skipdale's name links it to the time of the Scandinavian settlers, coming as it does from the West Saxon 'sceap' or the Old Norse 'scip' meaning sheep. The name simply means sheep valley, dale being the modern Yorkshire name for a valley. Like other towns in the area, Skipdale's economy has long depended on sheep and the woollen industry.

The Skipdale Commercial Canal was constructed to convey bales of wool into the heartland of West Yorkshire's mills. It joins the Leeds and Liverpool Canal near Keighley and although it is occasionally used by wool-bearing barges, it now features as a leisure amenity where it is popular with anglers and for boating holidays on cabin cruisers and canal boats.

Another major industry in Skipdale is brewing. At the beginning of the last century, there were some fifteen breweries in Skipdale, and by the turn of this century, five were still operating. Now, due to mergers and take-overs, only one family-owned brewery remains and this is called Ephraims Skipdale Ales. This was established in 1778 and continues to brew beer and ale by using the same water supply upon which the business was founded more than two centuries ago. The quality of the ale is due to the mineral content of the magnesian spring waters which occupy huge underground caverns beneath the surface of the surrounding fells, and these waters have been utilised for brewing since medieval times.

The Jacob family who founded the business could trace their ancestors to the Ephraim Mountains in central Palestine, described as one of the most fruitful areas of that region. Eli Jacob, the founder, saw similarities between the fells around Skipdale and the mountainous regions of his ancestral land and therefore called his ales by the name which still implies the very best of Yorkshire brews.

One of the unique features of the brewery is that it owns public houses and inns in many Yorkshire villages and Dales, but every one of these establishments is called the Woolpack Inn. This comes from the brewer's ancient links with the woollen industry of this region.

There are some splendid walks in the surrounding woodland, with many superb waterfalls on the moorland streams which flow down the steep fells. These are often called forces or fosses, while on the moors around Skipdale, the movement of glaciers, the passage of time and the effects of the bleak weather have sculpted strange shapes out of the rocks. Skipdale Sentinels, huge accumulations of windswept granite formations up to sixteen feet fall, are just one example and they can be reached by a public footpath which runs past St Gregory's Parish Church. It entails a walk of some twenty-five minutes.

The church, with its unique Jacobean rood screen and its pulpit carved from the timbers of Nelson's flagship, the *Victory*, should not be missed. Built in 1832, it occupies the site of several earlier churches, the one prior to this being destroyed by fire following some very direct and slanderous sermons by the then incumbent, Rev. Saul Ramshaw. Some of the contents of the church, such as several pews, the rood screen and the pulpit were salvaged, together with a fifteenth-century pewter chalice and some altar plate, and these can be seen in the present building.

The graveyard contains the tomb of Yorkshire's tallest woman, Eileen Butterworth, who died in 1896 aged twenty-two when she was seven feet two inches tall.

Skipdale Cattle Mart attracts dealers from all over the north of England, Scotland and Ireland, while sheep sales are a regular feature of the town's trading activities.

A vegetable and fruit market, which also sells household goods, is held every Wednesday in the outdoor market place, while the town centre is rich with modern shops and offices which cater for the requirements of the surrounding villages.

There is maypole dancing each year on May Day on the lawns of the castle, when a May Queen is crowned. Another annual event is the Mayor's Scramble when children under ten visit the Town Hall and scramble for pennies which are thrown from the upper windows. The number of pennies varies according to the age of the Mayor, with twelve pennies (one shilling in £.s.d. currency) being cast for each year of the Mayor's age. This is thought to have originated in the Sceapdael [*sic*] Dole in the twelfth century, when the poor of the town were given charitable donations from the Mayor's coffers.

THE SUGDEN FAMILY TREE

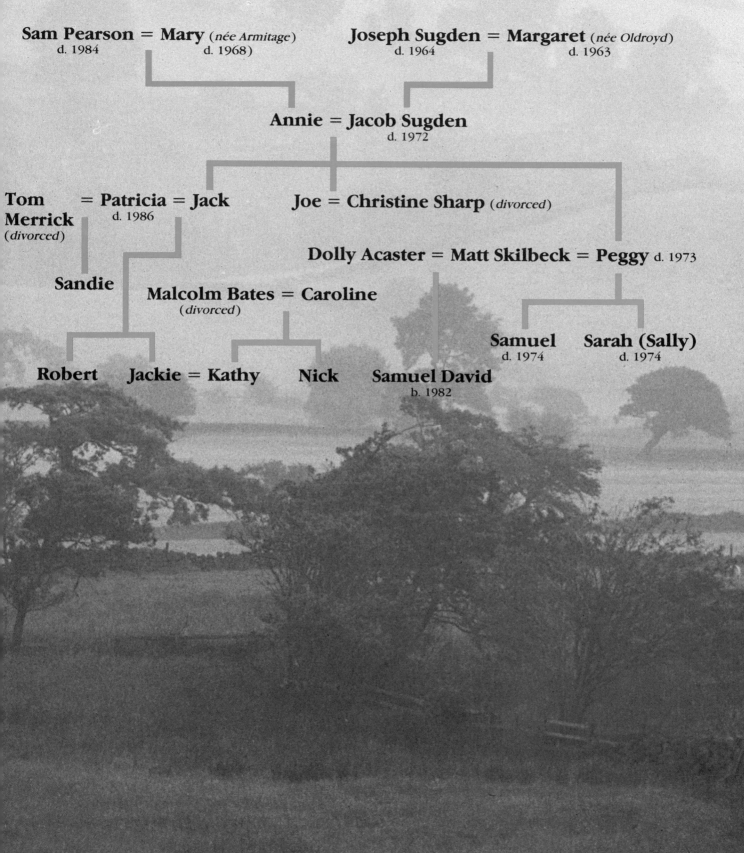

Sam Pearson = **Mary** (*née Armitage*)
d. 1984   d. 1968)

Joseph Sugden = **Margaret** (*née Oldroyd*)
d. 1964   d. 1963

Annie = **Jacob Sugden**
d. 1972

Tom = **Patricia** = **Jack**   **Joe** = **Christine Sharp** (*divorced*)
Merrick   d. 1986
(*divorced*)

Dolly Acaster = **Matt Skilbeck** = **Peggy** d. 1973

Sandie

Malcolm Bates = **Caroline**
(*divorced*)

Samuel   **Sarah (Sally)**
d. 1974   d. 1974

Robert   **Jackie** = **Kathy**   **Nick**   **Samuel David**
b. 1982

The first Beckindale wedding. Blacksmith Frank Blakey (Eric Allan) marries Janie Harker (Diane Grayson) at St Mary's, Beckindale. Jack Sugden was best man and Joe was a guest. The vicar was the Rev. Edward Ruskin.

After the heartbreak of losing Peggy and then the twins, Matt found happiness with Dolly Acaster (then played by Katherine Barker). They were married in Beckindale Parish Church.

Happy scenes at the wedding of Joe Sugden and Christine Sharp (Angela Cheyne). But Joe's happiness was not to last. Christine left him because she could not tolerate life as a farm labourer's wife in Beckindale and they were divorced.

When Jack wanted to marry divorcee Pat Merrick, the Rev. Donald Hinton refused to allow the wedding in his church because the marriage of a divorcee conflicted with his religious beliefs. So Jack and Pat were married in Hotten Registrar's Office.

When Jackie Merrick married Kathy Bates, a honeymoon followed in Tunisia (below). This was the first time that scenes from 'Emmerdale Farm' had been recorded overseas.

EMMERDALE FARM QUIZ

1 When was the first episode of 'Emmerdale Farm' transmitted?
2 Which actor played the part of Jack Sugden in that episode?
3 Who composed the title music for 'Emmerdale Farm'?
4 What is the name of the creator of 'Emmerdale Farm'?
5 Who got married in the first Beckindale wedding?
6 What were the names of Matt and Peggy Skilbeck's twins?
7 Who did Joe Sugden marry in 1974?
8 Who was 'Emmerdale Farm's' first woman producer?
9 What is Dolly Skilbeck's maiden name?
10 What is the full name of young Sam?
11 Who plays the part of Tom Merrick?
12 What is the Christian name of Seth Armstrong's wife?
13 What is the name of Henry Wilks's first home in Beckindale?
14 In addition to the Woolpack Inn, what is (a) the name of the other inn in Beckindale and (b) who is its landlord?
15 Who killed Harry Mowlem?
16 With whom did Jack Sugden have an affair shortly before Pat's tragic death?
17 What is the Christian name of Jack and Pat's youngest son?
18 In which of the YTV studios in Leeds is 'Emmerdale Farm' recorded?
19 What word is called to: (a) start recording a scene, (b) stop recording a scene, (c) stop recording for the day?
20 What is the Yorkshire name for a cow shed?
21 What breed are the cows on Emmerdale Farm?
22 What is the name of Seth Armstrong's dog?
23 What breed is Matt's sheepdog?
24 Which famous Dales brewery was founded in 1778?
25 What is the Christian name of Annie Sugden's late husband?
26 What was the joint title given in February 1986 to Henry Wilks and Amos Brearly?
27 What was the name of the magazine founded by Amos Brearly in January 1981?
28 What is the name of Henry Wilks's grandson?
29 Jackie Merrick once proposed to an Asian nurse. What was her name?
30 Who plays the part of Jackie's wife, Kathy?
31 Which 'Emmerdale Farm' actor became famous as Dr Rennie in 'Emergency Ward 10'?

Above left: *Cricket is a feature of every Yorkshire village and Beckindale is no exception. Here are some well-known players from a recent match.*

Above right: *The two Sams, young and old. Old Sam Pearson loved Matt and Dolly's son and was so proud that they shared the same Christian name. Had he been alive today, old Sam would have loved young Sam's attempts to play the recorder.*

32 In November 1973 a racehorse was named Emmerdale Farm. Who was its jockey?

33 PC 73 Derek Betts left Bradford City Police to become actor Martin Dale. What part does he now play in 'Emmerdale Farm'?

34 In 1987 'Emmerdale Farm' was recorded overseas for the first time and featured the honeymoon of Jackie and Kathy Merrick. In which country was this?

35 Which 'Emmerdale Farm' actress played Norma Ford in 'Coronation Street'?

36 In which other soap opera has Jean Rogers (Dolly Skilbeck) appeared?

37 In which Yorkshire Dales village was 'Emmerdale Farm' originally recorded?

38 Name the MP for the constituency in which Beckindale is situated.

39 Which 'Emmerdale Farm' actor is, in real life, a sheep farmer and registered sheep breeder?

40 'Emmerdale Farm' was never transmitted at Christmas until which year?

(*Answers on page 109*)

Chapter Five

Christmas at Beckindale

In bygone times, there was a tradition in the Yorkshire Dales that one's home should always be warm and welcoming at Christmas. No one should be turned away, not even a stranger. This dates to medieval times or even beyond, and it was based on the biblical story of Mary, Joseph and their baby Jesus who were turned away from the inn because there was no room for them.

The Dalesfolk have always said that such inhospitality would never have happened in Yorkshire and as a consequence (and just in case an unexpected caller could again be Christ), they ensure that there is a generous and warm welcome to any caller over the Christmas period, whether or not invited. If Mary, Joseph and their child Jesus should come to Yorkshire at Christmas, they will not be turned away from any cottage, house or farm, large or small, or from any Yorkshire inn, however crowded.

The preparations for Christmas begin early and great care is taken to make sure that everything is perfect for this most festive of occasions. The whole family joins in to help, for there is food to prepare, decorations to arrange, a Christmas tree to locate and install, holly, ivy and mistletoe to acquire, the Yule log to find in its storage place after last year, the presents to buy, drinks to plan and guests to invite.

Beckindale is among the hundreds of Yorkshire villages whose people strive to make this Christmas the happiest and most enjoyable, while the preparations at Emmerdale Farm are perhaps typical of any other farm or indeed any other house in North Yorkshire. Out of doors, the farm and the surrounding countryside appear to have come to rest. As December, with its dark nights and deepening chill, takes over from November, the landscape becomes dull and lifeless.

The trees and hedges have lost their foliage, the flowers have died and the birds have ceased their joyful singing that is such a feature of spring and summer. The colours of autumn have faded and the fields, recently ploughed, are a series of earthy colours which glisten in the weak sunshine. Many species of birds, who now flock for protection against the coming winter, visit these fields to seek grubs and worms while the farmer goes about his buildings and fields, repairing defective fences, walls, roofs and woodwork, cleaning ditches and at times preparing for early lambs.

His valuable cows may now be indoors, secure from the wintry weather which is a constant threat, but the sturdy sheep will remain outside spending their winter either in the fields or perhaps on the fells. Mountain sheep are bred for conditions of this kind, but the caring farmer or shepherd will visit them daily if conditions do become very severe, perhaps taking hay out to them on the fells or in the fields, or probing deep snow in case any have been buried by drifts.

There is no rest for the caring farmer at Christmas, but these early excursions and checks will ensure that a reasonably relaxed holiday is possible. And as the nights grow darker and the weather worsens, the man of the house will be gathering fuel for the roaring fires that will fill the chimneys over the twelve days of Christmas. He will be seeking logs that will burn merrily and with warmth, and the land will yield many of these. Emmerdale land will provide many warm logs for Jackie and Matt to gather; they will store these in a dry outbuilding until they are required, taking them into the house only when they are needed. In the orchard they will seek the fallen wood of fruit trees like the apple, the cherry and the pear, for this gives off a pleasant scent, and they will store some ash wood because this burns warmly whether it is green or weathered. Old oak gives off a warm blaze too, as does seasoned beechwood, hornbeam and chestnut. Birch burns too quickly while wood from the pine and other conifers spits out sparks as it blazes fiercely. Elmwood 'burns like churchyard mould' while the poplar creates an unpleasant smell.

While seeking these timbers, the men will be looking out for holly which bears bright red berries, for sprigs of yew or ivy which will adorn the houses and the church, and even for mistletoe, the parasite which grows on trees like the apple or the oak. There is not much wild mistletoe in North Yorkshire but Seth Armstrong reckons he knows a place where it grows in the woods of Home Farm Estate.

One of the essential logs for Christmas is the Yule log. Before his death, Grandad Pearson looked after the Yule log. He would always ensure that he located the partially burnt remains of last year's log which he had stored in a dry place. Then, for the new Yule log, Sam always chose a piece of weathered oak which he had put away as early as February so that it would be thoroughly dry in time for Christmas. He selected a piece about three feet long (although it could be up to four feet in length), and according to tradition, brought it into the house on Christmas Eve. He then placed the remains of the old log on the fire on Christmas Eve and before it had burnt away, ignited the new one from it. The new one should than be allowed to smoulder throughout the Christmas period, if possible up to Twelfth Night. A small part of the charred log was kept and this was stored until next year. Amos Brearly always has a Yule log at the Woolpack too, as do many other traditionalists in and around Beckindale.

For Annie Sugden, her most important consideration is the family Christmas dinner. She must make sure the entire family, Jack, Robert, and Joe, with Jackie and Kathy and also Matt, Dolly and little Sam are invited. She must also remember to invite Sandie and Mrs Bates who is now part of the family, and that means including her son, Nick. She might also include the vicar who is so often alone at Christmas. The menu is never a problem because, by tradition, the Emmerdale Christmas dinner always makes use of a fine Emmerdale goose.

But in the days before Christmas, she, Dolly and now Kathy will be busy plucking geese (the Yorkshire word for this is 'ploating' geese), for the Christmas markets and she has to accommodate her domestic work around the needs of the farm. Somehow, she must find time to make her Christmas cake, her Christmas pudding, her mince pies, ginger bread and apple pies, all of which are part of the fare for a traditional Yorkshire Christmas. Annie's recipes are renowned throughout Yorkshire, but she does love to follow one old custom when she mixes her Christmas pudding. She makes sure that most members of her family are present when she mixes her pudding on Stir-up Sunday; years ago, this was on Trinity Sunday, which is the Sunday after Whitsunday, but nowadays Annie mixes her pudding about a month before Christmas, although a Christmas pudding will keep for many weeks before use. But, in the manner of days gone by, she insists that every member of the family who is present must take a turn at stirring the contents and this must be done sun-wise, i.e. from east to west. This brings good fortune to the family, and each stirrer must make a wish as they take their turn with the spoon. Finally, before it is cooked, she will conceal a small silver coin in the pudding and the person who finds it will have good fortune during the coming year. This dates from the time when silver coins, blessed in church, were said to effect cures and bring good fortune, and so silver threepenny bits or sixpences were concealed in the pudding as good-luck charms.

The Christmas shopping for presents must be fitted into Annie's busy life and she will probably visit York, Harrogate or Leeds for this, although some Yorkshire folk now travel to London for a day in the city's shops. Sometimes a villager from Beckindale will organise a trip to the shops or to London to see the lights, but it is soon time to decorate the home.

By strict tradition, the Christmas decorations should not be put up until Christmas Eve, but many families now ignore this convention. They will adorn their houses much earlier, sometimes emulating the shops whose decorations brighten the towns in November or even earlier. With the darkness of winter upon the countryside, the colour added by decorations and bright lights adds a note of cheer and there seems to be no rule forbidding early decorations. Even the major establishments of the community like the church and the local inn will decorate their premises well before Christmas Eve.

This custom goes back to the Roman festival of Saturn which was held in December; at that time, greenery was used as a sign of continuing life, and before Christianity came to Britain evergreens were used at the winter solstice to bring the return of the dead vegetation and give life to crops. The people of Beckindale continue to make use of evergreens for their Christmas decorations while probably not appreciating their use as good-luck charms.

Holly is brought indoors as well as ivy, laurel, yew, bay, rosemary or indeed any available evergreen. Mistletoe, long regarded as a magical plant which makes enemies become friends, is also brought into the home, but by far the most important piece of evergreen is the Christmas tree. All over Beckindale, Norway spruce trees, large and small, are purchased from the owners of the surrounding forests or from markets nearby to be installed in the cottages and

Colourful scenes from recent Christmas pantomimes at Beckindale. See if you can recognise the characters in their costumes.

homes, when bright-coloured lights and gaudy baubles are added. Soon, every window in the village is aglow with these lights; Amos Brearly and Henry Wilks ensure that the Woolpack has a superior Christmas tree and sometimes a large one is erected outside the village hall; even the vicar installs one beside the altar in the parish church.

As the brightly lit church fills with the sound of the many voices of the choir practising their carols for Midnight Mass, the children of Beckindale grow more and more excited and more and more impatient as the magic hour of Christmas Eve approaches. These country children believe in Father Christmas, the white-bearded man in the red cloak who rides a sleigh hauled by reindeer from the snow wastes of the Arctic, and who somehow manages to supply every child in the world with a present on Christmas Eve. They prepare for his visit by being very, very good, by making sure the chimney is swept for his descent and ensuring mum has baked some mince pies for his supper.

For the families and businesses of Beckindale there are the inevitable last-minute arrangements and even panics; items of food to buy, last-minute presents to obtain for those who were overlooked, while Joe Sugden and Alan Turner must visit every home in the village, in the manner of the past squires of Beckindale, to give a small present to every villager – a brace of pheasants perhaps, a hare maybe or some other piece of game from the estate. There will be holly, too, for every villager (who in the time of the squires were all tenants) was given a bunch of fine holly as a gift, with a bottle of whisky for all the retired male tenants and a small bottle of perfume for their wives or retired lady workers. Joe and Alan, now jointly operating in the role of the new 'squire' must behave accordingly, and a Christmas bonus to all tenants and staff is expected from them.

Grandad Sam Pearson plays his flute during the children's Christmas nativity play at Beckindale.

Carol singing is very popular in Beckindale at Christmas and Annie Sugden, with members of her family, always joins in.

But they will not receive Yule candles from the villagers; those days have gone. Even within living memory, every tenant and worker would, at Christmas time, make the gift of a Yule candle to either the Lord of the Manor or to their employers. Yule candles were large and colourful and were sometimes very ornate; they cost very little, but they did look impressive and they did last for a long time. These would be welcomed by the squire who would light them and position them around the Hall or the tenants' room during the annual Christmas party for his workers and tenants.

The Verneys continued to receive Yule candles from some tenants until their departure from Beckindale Estate and with their departure the old custom died out.

Christmas Eve is a day of bustle and anticipation but there are some older folk in Beckindale who, even today, will never eat meat on Christmas Eve, and who will never drink alcohol. Instead, they eat spartan meals, perhaps an omelette or boiled egg, or even fish, and during the evening the traditional

105

Christmas dish of frumetty will be eaten by some Dales farmers and older folk. This is a type of porridge, the principal ingredient of which is pearled wheat, i.e. wheat which is still in the husk. The name varies from place to place, sometimes being known as furmety, frumenty or furmenty, but here in Beckindale, it is called frumetty.

Preparation begins the day before Christmas Eve when the pearled wheat is left overnight to soak in a bowl of water. This is known as creaving. Once the wheat has creaved (i.e. swollen due to the absorption of water), it can be cooked. This is done in a slow oven where the wheat is placed in a mixture of milk and water, one pint of mixed milk and water being used to every pound of wheat.

Slow cooking is essential and some allow up to three hours for this. The real tradition is to eat it hot at midnight when it is like a thick gruel or heavy milk pudding, and flavouring is added to taste. The flavourings can be either liqueurs, rum, brandy, fruit of various sorts such as raisins, sultanas or currants, spices of all kinds such as nutmeg or cinnamon or something as simple as sugar or honey. The flavouring is simply stirred in according to taste.

It is wise to allow the dried fruit time to soften before incorporating it, but the frumetty can be served either hot or cold, sometimes with cream on top. Not everyone likes frumetty, for it was originally a kind of penance on the eve of Christmas but, by tradition, it should be eaten by the family before a roaring log fire, along with other Christmas delicacies like mince pies, ginger bread and apple pie and cheese, or perhaps a little of each!

Before Midnight Mass became a regular feature of the modern Christmas, frumetty was eaten at midnight, after which the presents were given and opened. Some families would eat their frumetty during the late evening, however, around nine o'clock, so that the children could go to bed to await Father Christmas, following which the presents were opened next morning. Now that many Beckindale families go to the Christmas Midnight Mass, frumetty is sometimes eaten upon their return home with perhaps a glass of something rather special!

Some children, and indeed some adults, will sneak into the mistle at farms like Emmerdale hoping to see the cattle on their knees. There is an ancient tradition that the flocks of sheep and domestic animals like cows and horses, turn to the east and fall to their knees at midnight on Christmas Eve, the traditional hour of Christ's birth. Some even believe the cattle weep at this time. But no human must witness these secret rituals, although some farmers would visit their mistles on Christmas Eve to toast the health of the animals during the coming year.

From midnight, therefore, it is Christmas Day, a time of magic for children and adults alike, and all that is needed is a touch of snow. Here in the Yorkshire Dales, there can be seasonal falls of snow around Christmas time when the beautiful countryside is given a coverlet of pure white which glistens in the light of the moon. The Yorkshire folk call this a 'strinkling' of snow, a lovely old word which evokes such a charming picture of the dale. A sharp frost will add a touch of glitter to the snow, too, so that the pines growing naturally on the fells look like forests of Christmas trees in the rays of the sun or by the light of the moon, while the fields and ranging moorlands on the Pennines are

When Amos won a pair of turkeys in a Christmas raffle, no one told him the birds were still alive!

as huge iced cakes. At dawn on Christmas morning, the birds and animals make tracks in the snow as the people settle down to this most joyous of family occasions.

For the tiny children like Sam Skilbeck and Robert Sugden, the magic of the day is the mysterious arrival of Father Christmas. With his team of reindeer and his heavily laden sleigh, he flies across the world, descending the chimneys of our homes to deliver his surprises. Sam has now reached the age when he lies awake on Christmas Eve in the hope he will catch sight of this famous visitor, but so far he has failed – but the presents always come to his bedside.

Robert is still too young to understand fully the magic of this season, but he loves to return to Emmerdale with his father to share in the happiness that the day creates. The fire in the parlour is always lit and a huge Yule log smoulders away throughout the holiday; during the morning, before the family Christmas dinner, people call and have a drink with friends and perhaps a piece of ginger bread and cheese.

Christmas dinner, the year's most celebratory meal, occupies the family during the morning too; everyone helps but no one can match Annie's expertise and experience in producing the finest of dinners. The goose, which will have been reared on the farm, will be cooked to perfection, and there will be masses of other vegetables from the farm garden – sprouts, potatoes (both roast and mashed), carrots, peas with Annie's own gravy and all the trimmings of the very best of Yorkshire Christmas dinners. The main course will be preceded by hot soup, and afterwards there will be Annie's famous Christmas pudding.

This will be made to the recipe that has been handed down from mother to daughter for generations. Thick white rum sauce will accompany it and attempts will be made to ignite the cup of brandy that will be poured upon the pudding. Wine will flow during the meal; sometimes crackers will be pulled and fancy paper hats worn as the meal progresses, with glasses being raised and the health of everyone is drunk with deep love and respect for one another. Some will turn to day dreaming during this happy occasion, Kathy and Jackie in particular, as they make a wish that soon they will have a home of their own.

After the meal, the family will listen to the Queen's Christmas broadcast, a tradition insisted upon by Grandad when he was alive, and all will help with the chore of washing up as Annie relaxes before the blazing fire, watching her grandchildren play with their new toys and basking in the glow of happiness that Christmas has brought to Emmerdale yet again.

Later in the day, perhaps even as late as the evening, the cake will be cut. The huge dinner has left no room for the cake, and so it will be cut when it can be appreciated; everyone will receive a slice along with their favourite drink and toasts will be drunk yet again. Slices of the cake will be retained for sending to absent friends and relations, and pieces will be kept for unexpected callers and for those who have helped the Sugdens during the year – the vet, for example, the policeman, the postman and the newspaper boy, the salesmen and other farming advisers who have called so regularly.

Distant friends and relatives will be telephoned to express seasonal good wishes and the day will fade into a happy and relaxed occasion of good food, fine wine, the warmth of a loving family and the cheerful blaze of a log fire beneath the colourful array of decorations and Christmas lights.

All too soon it will be over. As the darkness descends in late afternoon, the excitement has left everyone weary and drained; the children are prepared for bed as the adults want nothing more than to relax before the fire with their own thoughts and impressions.

Tomorrow will be Boxing Day, a time for fox hunting in the countryside and playing football or visiting one of the many sports events in the region. And with the activities of Boxing Day, often combined with long walks in the Dales and upon the fells for those who do not favour the available sports, the central part of the family Christmas will be over.

But for Beckindale village, there will be more to follow; there will be the annual Christmas pantomime in the village hall, the playschool's party and the trip organised for the old folks to either Leeds or Bradford to see a professional pantomime or variety show.

In the countryside beyond the village, however, when Christmas is over the farmers will return to their labours as winter intensifies; there could be lambs very soon and the stocks of fodder and bedding will have to be checked very carefully. There will be ditches to clear out, fences to repair, gates to mend and other essential maintenance work to complete. . . .

For some in Beckindale, however, Christmas can be a lonely time. The vicar, the Rev. Donald Hinton, sometimes finds himself feeling very isolated at Christmas. Clive, his son, is working overseas and Barbara, his daughter, leads her own life away from Beckindale. Unless a parishioner invites him for Christmas dinner he could spend the day alone after his Christmas morning service, eating in the silence and misery of the huge and empty vicarage.

Donald Hinton always enjoys the activity before Christmas – helping with the decorating of the church with its greenery, lights and candles, the ever-lasting music of the carols and the other sacred music of the Christmas period, the excitement and splendour of his Midnight Mass and the presents or cards he receives. And after Christmas he invariably gets involved with the village pantomime, usually in the capacity of producer with all the worry and hard work that such a role involves. Happily, Annie Sugden never forgets him and he is a regular guest at her magnificent Christmas dinner table.

Another lonely soul is Alan Turner. Even his secretary Mrs Bates is now part of the Emmerdale family which means he is liable to spend Christmas by himself; sometimes, in the past, Mrs Bates has invited him to join her family. His son Terence is not very considerate, rarely bothering to send a card.

However, he is fortunate that his former wife, Jill, from whom he is divorced, does invite him to Manchester for Christmas whenever he cares to make the trip.

But in his new business he is hoping to attact wealthy guests to Home Farm Estate over the Christmas period, when he will arrange traditional fare and hospitality for them. He imagines himself hosting his guests before a roaring log fire in the vast rooms of Home Farm, wining and dining them with the choicest of dishes and the very best of wines and liqueurs, a truly Yorkshire

Answers to Quiz on page 99

1 16 October 1972
2 Andrew Burt
3 Tony Hatch
4 Kevin Laffan
5 Blacksmith Frank Blakey and Janie Harker
6 Sam and Sally
7 Christine Sharp
8 Anne Gibbons
9 Acaster
10 Samuel David Skilbeck
11 Jack Carr
12 Meg
13 Inglebrook
14 (a) The Malt Shovel, (b) Ernie Shuttleworth
15 Derek Warner
16 Karen Moore
17 Robert
18 Studio 3
19 (a) Action, (b) Cut, (c) Wrap
20 Mistle
21 Friesians

22 Smokey
23 A Border Collie
24 Ephraims Skipdale Ales
25 Jacob
26 Pipemen of the Year
27 The Beckindale Bugle (it did not survive)
28 Niccolo Rossetti
29 Sita Sharma
30 Malandra Burrows
31 Richard Thorp (who plays Alan Turner)
32 Frazer Hines (who plays Joe Sugden)
33 Police Sergeant Ian MacArthur
34 Tunisia
35 Diana Davies
36 'Crossroads'
37 Arncliffe
38 Mrs Amelia Ridgely-Jones
39 Peter Alexander (who plays Phil Pearce)
40 1988

Christmas with an affable and generous host. He hopes to attract a carefully selected gathering of top-quality guests, for they will be a solution to his Christmas loneliness, but will his dreams come true?

At the Woolpack Inn, Amos and Henry are far too busy to be lonely. Their Christmas starts early, for they must select and purchase sufficient drink of every kind to cater for the varied tastes of the customers, and there is a range of Christmas fare to provide, such as mince pies, nuts of all kinds and ginger bread to offer the customers with slices of best Wensleydale cheese – with the compliments of the proprietors.

The inn is decorated in style with coloured lights along the outside front wall and very fashionable streamers within. Amos ensures there is lots of greenery – holly, ivy and mistletoe, of course! And a fine Christmas tree.

As the locals realise, Amos is highly conscious of the role played by an inn during that very first Christmas and he wants to be sure that everyone who visits the Woolpack is given the warmest of welcomes. Among the delights he has arranged for his regulars is the annual Christmas Draw for charity, the Boxing Day Darts and Domino competition between the regulars of the Woolpack and those of the rival licensed establishment in Beckindale, whose name Amos does not like to mention, and a five-a-side football knock-out competition between teams from Beckindale and district.

In a small cottage in Demdyke Row, Mrs Meg Armstrong is able to keep an eye on her wandering husband, Seth. Christmas dinner is the one occasion when she knows where to find him; he has never missed his Christmas dinner and he always carves the turkey with the enjoyment of someone about to partake in a banquet.

He always buys Meg a brooch for Christmas and she always buys him a bottle of finest malt whisky, one of his favourite drinks other than beer. He does help around the house during the preparations for dinner, although he never misses a quick dash up to the Woolpack for a couple of pints of best bitter, before returning to Meg for the rest of the day. And after dinner, he sleeps.

But at least Seth Armstrong has Christmas Day at home.

For a few days after Christmas, a holiday atmosphere pervades Beckindale although the work of the farm and the activities in the countryside cannot stop. There is no holiday for the cattle and sheep of the Dales, no break in routine for those whose work involves a continuing responsibility for others whether at home or elsewhere, and no break for those who struggle so hard to ensure that their family, colleagues, friends and customers enjoy a happy Christmas.

In Beckindale, Christmas continues until Twelfth Night, otherwise known as the Eve of the Epiphany which is 5 January. On that day, the decorations must be taken down and the greenery removed from the houses and other places. The Christmas tree must be stripped of its baubles and tinsel and taken into the garden for disposal. Some think it is unlucky to burn it, and so it is allowed to rot away; some will obtain trees with roots on them, so they can be planted for another year.

The first Monday after Twelfth Night is Plough Monday when work on the farm resumes in earnest.

Chapter Six
The Cast

SHEILA MERCIER
(*Annie Sugden*)

Sheila Mercier has played Annie Sugden since the beginning of 'Emmerdale Farm'.

Sheila Mercier has enjoyed a lifelong interest in acting and feels this is due to her family's love of the theatre. Her mother had a fine singing voice and enjoyed organising charity shows for the church, while her ship-owner father helped by making the scenery.

Sheila is the sister of actor Brian Rix and at home the children were expected to perform a party piece during the family's frequent social gatherings. This gave her confidence in front of an audience and nurtured her love of acting.

At drama school she came to the notice of Sir Donald Wolfit who invited her to join his company. She then toured the country with Sir Donald until the Second World War intervened. Sheila joined the WAAF

and produced shows on every camp at which she served. When the war was over, she played in repertory all over Britain, including several of the famous Whitehall farces which featured her brother.

Sheila has played Annie Sugden since the beginning of 'Emmerdale Farm', and is one of the five remaining members of the original cast.

CLIVE HORNBY
(*Jack Sugden*)

Tall, dark and distinctive, Clive Hornby has played the part of Jack since the more mature Jack's permanent return to Emmerdale. The character of Jack has been in the serial since the beginning, but has been played by two actors; Clive had the difficult task of portraying Jack after Andrew Burt, and he did so after one of Jack's long absences, a feature of the storyline that made the transition acceptable to the viewers.

Liverpool-born Clive joined the Liverpool Playhouse Theatre as Assistant Stage Manager. Here he discovered the appeal of the theatre and spent three years at the London Academy of Music and Dramatic Art. Before joining 'Emmerdale Farm', Clive worked in children's theatre, repertory and TV, and it was while acting in Agatha Christie's play

Murder at the Vicarage at the Fortune Theatre, London, that he was offered the part of Jack Sugden.

One aspect of the role has changed Clive's personal life; he met Helen Weir who played one of his earlier loves and later his wife, Pat Sugden, the former Mrs Tom Merrick. As they worked together, they fell in love – and they became Mr and Mrs Hornby as well as Mr and Mrs Sugden. In December 1985 their son Thomas was born.

Actor Jack Carr plays the roguish Tom Merrick.

FRAZER HINES
(*Joe Sugden*)

It was at the point when Joe went to France to work for NY Estates in 1983 that Frazer Hines left 'Emmerdale Farm'. In the part of Joe Sugden, a bright and breezy personality, Frazer had been with 'Emmerdale' since the series started and is one of the five remaining original members of the cast.

Rumours of his impending departure created speculation that the character of Joe was to be killed off and this prompted shoals of letters from upset fans. But it was not so.

'I wanted a break,' Frazer said. 'I needed an opportunity for a period of assessment of my own life. I'd just got married and the trips down the M1 to see my wife were getting tedious. It was agreed that my wish for a change would coincide with a similar break in the storyline.'

And so, with Annie in tears and sorrowing at the departure of her youngest son, Joe Sugden left Beckindale to live and work in France.

Frazer Hines was born at Horsforth near Leeds in Yorkshire and has been in showbusiness since he was eight years old. By the age of fifteen he had appeared in half a dozen films, and older viewers may recall him as Jamie, the somewhat truculent Scots assistant to Dr Who in the early stories of the time-travelling doctor and his Tardis.

During his break from 'Emmerdale Farm' he raced a little, acted a little and underwent a deep personal sadness in June 1984 with the end of his marriage to actress Gemma Craven.

But Joe's popularity paved the way for the return of Frazer Hines to 'Emmerdale Farm'; he reappeared on our screens on 25 March 1986 when Joe came back to Beckindale for a holiday. He soon learned there was a vacancy in the post of Regional Manager of NY Estates. Joe applied and was appointed – and so became Alan Turner's boss.

FREDERICK PYNE
(Matt Skilbeck)

Born in London, Freddie was brought up near the borders of Cambridgeshire and Hertfordshire and has a deep affection for that part of England. As a youngster, he spent some time on a farm which developed his love of the land.

At first he had decided upon a career in teaching, but when he won a place at the Royal Academy of Dramatic Art he decided that acting would be his life. He worked in many repertory companies throughout Britain and among those with whom he has worked while at the National Theatre and the Royal Court are Sir Laurence Olivier, Sir John Mills, Sir John Gielgud and Sir Tyrone Guthrie. He treasures memories of his engagements with the National Theatre at the Old Vic. In 1987 he completed a ten-week national tour with *Billy Liar*, playing the father. Among his TV roles are those in 'Dixon of Dock Green', 'Macbeth' and 'Justice'.

JEAN ROGERS
(Dolly Skilbeck)

Jean Rogers as Dolly Skilbeck.

Born in Worthing, Jean was only nine when she told her parents that she wanted to be an actress. Her parents perhaps encouraged this by taking her to the cinema every Friday night, and she became enthralled by the world of film and theatre. To further her ambition, she took lessons in elocution, drama, ballet and singing and volunteered for school plays and music festivals. At fifteen she tried to enrol at drama school but was rejected due to her age, so she tried again at seventeen and was accepted by the Guildhall School of Drama.

Jean has worked with the National Theatre and Chichester Festival Theatre as well as doing repertory work in Coventry and Farnham. She spent three years presenting the BBC TV programme 'Watch' and has more than 1,500 broadcasts to her credit, including seven years with 'Listen with Mother'. She has appeared in many TV productions including 'George and Mildred', 'Crossroads', 'General Hospital' and 'Emergency Ward 10'. She has often been the principal boy in pantomime, while in some of her radio work she has been cast as a boy because, as she says, 'My voice can sound light and boyish on radio.'

BENJAMIN WHITEHEAD
(Sam Skilbeck)

Two junior members of the 'Emmerdale' cast – Richard Smith who plays Robert Sugden (left) and Benjamin Whitehead who plays young Sam Skilbeck.

The selection of Benjamin Whitehead for the part of young Sam arose by pure chance. Jean Rogers was travelling on a train when she was recognised by a Mrs Lee, an ardent follower of the 'Emmerdale' story. She lived at Otley, not far from some of the locations used for outside recording.

In the storyline Dolly was pregnant and this was mentioned during the chat between Jean and Mrs Lee; Jean mentioned that the producer was presently seeking a baby to play the part of young Sam whereupon Mrs Lee said her friend Sue Whitehead was expecting a baby in October. As this date coincided with the anticipated birth of young Sam, Jean suggested that Mrs Whitehead write to the 'Emmerdale' office.

But Mrs Lee had no intention of risking shyness in her friend, so she wrote instead and told her friend after the letter had been posted. The outcome was that Sue Whitehead was invited to the offices of Yorkshire Television to discuss the possibility of her son playing the part of young Sam. Baby Benjamin was only a week old at that interview but he got the part!

Martin Dale in his role as Sergeant Ian MacArthur.

RONALD MAGILL
(*Amos Brearly*)

Amos is played to perfection by Ronnie Magill, one of the five original members of the cast, and his famous whiskers have become Amos's trademark, an effect introduced almost by chance.

'When I auditioned for the part,' said Ronnie, 'I had come directly from a play set in Edwardian times when these kind of whiskers were the height of fashion. When I got the part, I expected I'd have to shave them off, but was told they were perfect for Amos Brearly.'

Born in Hull, Ronnie's parents were schoolteachers but his constant love has been the theatre. During the Second World War, when he was in the Royal Corps of Signals, he found an outlet for his talents. He became involved in shows for the army, joining Stars in Battledress, and later built a theatre in Egypt where he produced plays. He is a very well-read man and has adapted two plays by Goldoni, *Mine Hostess* and *The Servant of Two Masters*. He has also adapted Molière's *The Miser* and *Treasure Island*, and has written the book of a musical of *Christmas Carol*.

For nine years, he was a director and actor at the Nottingham Playhouse and has starred at the Bristol Old Vic as Willie Loman in Arthur Miller's *Death of a Salesman* and as Crocker Harris in *The Browning Version*. He also appeared in *Julius Caesar* with Charlton Heston and his TV roles include parts in 'Special Branch' and 'Parkin's Patch'.

Johnny Caesar as Bill Middleton, one of the employees of Home Farm Estates.

ARTHUR PENTELOW
(*Henry Wilks*)

Henry Wilks has been part of the 'Emmerdale Farm' story since the beginning and Arthur Pentelow is one of the five remaining members of the original cast.

Although he enjoyed playing Shakespeare at Grammar School and in amateur theatre, Arthur Pentelow became a police cadet in his native

Rochdale but found his career plans interrupted by the Second World War. After serving in Normandy, followed by a year's teaching, he joined the new Bradford Drama School, and while seeking theatrical work he supplemented his income by doing odd jobs such as selling ice cream or sliced bread, and even taking washing to the laundry for overworked housewives!

He has acted in many radio plays and his TV appearances include 'Z-Cars', 'The Troubleshooters', 'United', 'Emergency Ward 10', 'Hadleigh', 'Coronation Street' and many other dramas including 'Armchair Theatre' and 'Play for Today'. His film roles include *The Peace Game*, *Privilege* and *Charlie Bubbles*.

Julia Chambers played the beautiful vet, Ruth Pennington, with whom Joe had a wonderful romance . . .

HUGH MANNING
(*The Reverend Donald Hinton*)

Hugh Manning was President of Equity, the actors' union, and served on the Executive Council for twenty years. He is currently one of the four trustees of Equity. He is also chairman of two theatrical trusts as well as being on the board of a drama school and involved in various other committees connected with the arts. He was a founder member of 'Arts for Labour', an advisory group on the arts for the Labour Party.

One of his earlier and widely known

113

roles was with Kathleen Harrison in 'Mrs Thursday', written by Ted Willis; this followed 'The Sullivan Brothers' also written by Ted Willis, in which he played a barrister, but Hugh Manning has travelled the world to act. He has played Shakespeare in India – his favourite country outside England – and has toured America in various plays. He has been in almost every country in the world, two notable exceptions being China and South America.

Hugh Manning has performed in more than twenty Shakespearean plays and has played the lead in a number of London's West End theatres. One of his happiest memories was working with Noel Coward in *The Apple Cart* at the Haymarket Theatre, London, in Coronation Year, 1953.

Fans will recognise him from other TV productions like 'The Avengers', 'Sergeant Cork' and 'Poldark' and he has also worked in one-man shows, one of which was 'Song of the Lion'. His latest film was the highly acclaimed *The Elephant Man*.

JANE HUTCHESON
(*Sandie Merrick*)

Phil Pearce is played by Peter Alexander. Here he is with Sandie Merrick (Jane Hutcheson) and Ellie the pup.

Jane Hutcheson joined 'Emmerdale Farm' in 1980 in the role of Sandie Merrick, the daughter of Tom and Pat Merrick.

Born in Stockport, Jane started her

acting career as a child and won several awards in amateur dramatic competitions. At only fourteen, she was principal girl in *Sleeping Beauty* and her enjoyable TV début came in the 'Ken Dodd Show' when, as a member of a teenage audience, she had to throw eggs and tomatoes at Ken and take part in disco dancing with the Diddy Men. She also won parts in 'Coronation Street', 'Family at War' and 'How We Used To Live', but, rather like her fictional character, Sandie Merrick, Jane did not ignore her academic work. She gained her 'A' levels and went to Birmingham University where she studied drama, following which she worked in repertory in Britain and with an English-speaking theatre company in France.

Jane was working with a repertory company in Bolton when she received the offer of the part of Sandie Merrick in 'Emmerdale Farm' and she accepted without hesitation.

'I really enjoy the Outside Broadcast work which is so much a part of "Emmerdale Farm",' Jane says. 'I love the outdoors and enjoy activities like badminton, horse-riding, swimming and work-outs in a local gym.'

IAN SHARROCK
(*Jackie Merrick*)

Ian Sharrock plays Jackie Merrick.

For Ian Sharrock, work on 'Emmerdale Farm' is almost like working next door. Before his marriage he lived with his parents at Darley near Harrogate, only a few

miles from the fictitious Emmerdale Farm and for a time worked on odd jobs and as a furniture salesman in Harrogate. But acting has always been his first love and he joined the Corona Drama School when he was twelve.

He appeared in the Walt Disney film *Candleshoe* with Jodi Foster and David Niven, played Smike in a TV musical and appeared with Danny Kaye and Mia Farrow in an ATV spectacular. He has acted in more than thirty radio plays and his Yorkshire TV début came with a leading role in 'Games', a series of six plays starring Geoffrey Palmer and Barbara Leigh Hunt.

In 1985 Ian and his wife, Pam, were married at the Roman Catholic Cathedral in Leeds and 4,000 Emmerdale fans arrived to witness the event! And then in January 1986 his daughter Natalie Clare was born, with a baby son, William Ian, following in May 1988.

Drew Dawson plays the part of Jock MacDonald.

MALANDRA BURROWS
(*Kathy Merrick, née Bates*)

Born in Liverpool, where she still lives, Malandra was only four when she knew she wanted to be an actress. She was chosen to present a posy to Dame Margot Fonteyn during a visit to a dancing school; the renowned ballerina picked up the tiny blonde girl with the blue eyes and asked, 'Would you like to be a dancer when you grow up?' to which Malandra replied, 'No,

I want to be an actress like you!'

She made her TV début on Yorkshire TV's 'Junior Showtime' when she was six and regularly appeared as a dancer and singer. At nine, she became the youngest-ever 'New Faces' winner, and to pursue her ambition Malandra worked hard at school, gaining nine 'O' levels. But instead of going to university as her parents and teachers had hoped, she opted for a course at the Mabel Fletcher Drama School. This led to fringe theatre work in productions like *Dracula* and *Frankenstein*, but she was soon offered a glamorous part in 'Brookside' on Channel 4. Within a very short time there came the offer from 'Emmerdale Farm' which she accepted in 1986. During the Christmas 1987/88 season, she played Snow White in a record-breaking pantomime.

Malandra Burrows plays Kathy Merrick (née Bates).

STAN RICHARDS
(*Seth Armstrong*)

The lovable but roguish character of Seth owes much to the acting skills of Stan Richards, but Stan still considers himself a musician and comedian rather than an actor. After school he worked as a civil servant and then joined the National Coal Board, working as a musician in his spare time. Eventually the hectic pace of his double life became such that in the 1960s he decided to become a full-time musician, even though he had a wife and three young children to support.

Because he has such an irrepressible sense of fun, Stan began to introduce humour into his musical act, and the outcome was that his comedy routine became more popular than his music. By 1968 his solo act was one of the most popular in the demanding world of northern clubs. It was this exposure that led him into acting roles, and he appeared in 'Coronation Street', 'All Creatures Great and Small', 'Last of the Summer Wine' and many other productions.

RICHARD THORP
(*Alan Turner*)

Richard Thorp's very successful portrayal of the nasty Alan Turner has caused him problems; someone once slashed the tyres of his Range Rover and left a note to say how they loathed him, while on another occasion some diners got up and walked out of a restaurant when he walked in. Fortunately, Richard sees this as a tribute to his acting ability, although it does show how some viewers cannot distinguish fact from fiction. list of credits as an actor, including parts in *The Dam Busters*, 'The Barrets of Wimpole Street', 'Family at War', 'The Cedar Tree', 'To The Manor Born', and the lead in *Murder at the Vicarage* on stage in the West End of London. In the 1960s he was famous as Dr Rennie in 'Emergency Ward 10'.

He now lives with his wife, Noola, in a splendid house in the Yorkshire Dales where he can indulge in a most unlikely passion – collecting and riding powerful motorcycles.

DIANA DAVIES
(*Mrs Caroline Bates*)

Diana Davies lives in Manchester and crosses the Pennines when required for recording at Yorkshire TV. Her father was a big-band musician who felt showbusiness was an unreliable and unglamorous profession, and he tried unsuccessfully to dissuade her from becoming an actress. When she realised just how determined she was, he relented and gave her every support.

She is no stranger to dramatic serials like 'Emmerdale Farm', for she played Norma Ford in 'Coronation Street' and has starred in 'Family at War'. Her other TV credits include 'Juliet Bravo', 'Willie's Last Stand' and 'How We Used to Live'. In addition she has appeared on the stages of theatres like Liverpool's Everyman Theatre, the Nottingham Playhouse and the Duke of York Theatre in London.

Diana Davies as Mrs Caroline Bates.

TONY PITTS
(*Archie Brooks*)

Tony Pitts' working life began as a truck mechanic in Sheffield but he had often considered acting and was given the lead part in *Looks and Smiles* made by Ken Loach who also made the film *Kes*. This persuaded him to give up his mechanic's job for a career in acting and after only a month out of work he was offered a role in Granada TV's 'Bingo'.

This was followed by a theatre tour with Trevor Griffiths's *Oi for England* and an appearance in the BBC's 'Play for Today' with Charles Dance and Cyril Cusack. He was shortlisted to the final two for the part of Terry Duckworth in 'Coronation Street' and has played a psychopathic killer in the BBC's 'Film on Two'.

The realistic behaviour and speech which Tony uses is based upon his own twenty-one-year-old brother, Mark, who is chairman of the Socialist Workers' Party in Sheffield. The earrings are part of Tony's own character for he wears them in real life.

Tony Pitts as Archie Brooks.

CY CHADWICK
(*Nick Bates*)

Cy Chadwick as Nick Bates.

Cy Chadwick's interest in the theatre started at the age of nine, and when he was thirteen he attended a theatrical school to study dance and drama. When Yorkshire TV was casting for its popular programme 'The Book Tower', Cy secured the part of Johnny Plakham which was his first TV role. Afterwards he was asked to take part in Yorkshire TV's 'How We Used To Live', a children's programme, and he secured several parts in amateur productions with some voice-over parts on radio.

Cy left school at sixteen and admits his acting ambitions always took precedence over his academic work. But upon leaving school he got the part of Jason Webber in the film *On The Boat* which was shown on German TV, and quickly found himself auditioning for the part of Nick Bates in 'Emmerdale Farm'.

Cy got the part and joined the 'Emmerdale Farm' cast in September 1985.

TOKE TOWNLEY
(*Grandad Pearson*)

Grandad Sam Pearson as played by the late Toke Townley.

On the wall of the Green Room used by the 'Emmerdale Farm' cast for their rest periods is a rather aged black-and-white photograph of a very young actor called Toke Townley. It is matched by a larger and more recent colour photograph of Sam Pearson, which stands on the mantelpiece at Emmerdale Farm.

There is half a century or more between these two pictures but they are of the same person for the lovable Toke Townley played the equally lovable Grandad in the 'Emmerdale Farm' serial.

Grandad was a gentle man who loved the countryside and who followed an honest and uncomplicated life where expectations were low but standards were high. He loved the lore and traditions of the countryside, and he expected strict and almost Puritan

standards from his family. Grandad was loved by everyone, viewers, cast and production crew alike.

Toke Townley, on the other hand, did not like the countryside for he was a townsman, but a townsman who loved his own company and lived most of the time in an hotel, and yet he was on first-name terms with almost everyone at Yorkshire TV. Toke was his real name, and one of his hobbies was good music, either from listening to records or by playing the flute and the recorder, a skill he sometimes used as Grandad during the Beckindale Christmas pantomime or at the playschool children's party.

Many viewers will remember the flower that Sam wore in his buttonhole. This happened because one day in 1977 Sam picked a buttercup and slipped it into his buttonhole. Producer Michael Glynn felt that as Sam loved flowers it would make a nice touch if he wore it every day. And so from that time Sam wore a flower of some kind in his buttonhole.

But, sadly, Toke died very suddenly. In 1984 he collapsed while out shopping and was taken into hospital for a check-up. He died during the night.

He is sadly missed by everyone associated with 'Emmerdale Farm', but his memory lives on, both as the unique Toke Townley and as the delightful Grandad Sam Pearson.

Postscript

By Stuart Doughty – Producer

I am the eighth producer to be entrusted with looking after 'Emmerdale Farm' and I am conscious that, although television is a very ephemeral medium, the programme has become a national institution.

On 5 January 1988 'Emmerdale Farm' was, for the first time, transmitted all over the UK at the same time on the same day – something that has taken fifteen years to achieve! Also in 1988, 'Emmerdale Farm' will be transmitted in Christmas week for the first time.

This seems a good time, therefore, to bring out *The Official Companion* – a book which I welcome as long overdue.

Unlike 'Dallas' and 'Dynasty' in America, British soap operas are about ordinary people – you and me, your mum and my mum – not about glamour queens and millionaires. British soaps are about everyday things: going to work, being unemployed, falling in love, splitting up, rowing with your parents, buying a car, painting the kitchen ... births, marriages and deaths (though not always in that order!).

This is part of the appeal of programmes like 'Emmerdale Farm': they are about situations which many of us are familiar with, and about problems which many of us have been through. We can sympathise with the characters we see on screen, and grow to love them, as many millions of you have grown to love the Sugdens, the Skilbecks and the Merricks.

It is, then, the stories and the chatactcrs which make 'Emmerdale Farm' as popular as it is.

Some people ask me whether 'Emmerdale Farm' is the *only* programme I work on; others may wonder whether producing a soap is really a job for a grown man. I can assure you that producing 'Emmerdale Farm' not only fills most of my waking hours (and some of my sleeping ones!) but also that it is endlessly fascinating trying to weave our wonderful characters into stories that will entertain and amuse 11,000,000 viewers twice a week.

I hope you have enjoyed this *Official Companion*, and I hope you'll keep watching to see what happens next ... I know I will!

Stuart Doughty, Producer of 'Emmerdale Farm'.